Heralding
Article 25

Heralding
Article 25
A people's
strategy
for world
transformation

Mohammed Mesbahi

Matador
9 Priory Business Park,
Wistow Road, Kibworth Beauchamp,
Leicestershire. LE8 0RX
Tel: 0116 279 2299
Email: books@troubador.co.uk
Web: www.troubador.co.uk/matador
Twitter: @matadorbooks

Cover Artwork: Arthimedes/Shutterstock.com

ISBN 978 1785891 410

British Library Cataloguing in Publication Data.
A catalogue record for this book is available from the British Library.

Printed and bound by CPI Group (UK) Ltd, Croydon, CR0 4YY
Typeset in 11pt Adobe Garamond Pro by Troubador Publishing Ltd, Leicester, UK

Matador is an imprint of Troubador Publishing Ltd

The time has come when we must demonstrate in our millions not against this or that, but on the basis of the goodwill and compassion that defines who we truly are. For within each and every human heart is embedded the love and wisdom of all humanity.

– Mohammed Mesbahi

Contents

Introduction

The book you are about to read is somewhat different from most other publications on politics, economics or philosophy, for which reason some words of introduction may be useful to help indicate the best approach to studying this uncommon discourse. Indeed this unique and pioneering book with its five interrelated parts originated in the form of actual dialogues between the author, Mohammed Mesbahi, and other members of the civil society organisation he founded in 2003, known as Share The World's Resources (STWR).[1] The ongoing dialogues have been converted into a series of publications under the title *Studies on the Principle of Sharing*, which together examine world problems from psychological and spiritual as well as social, economic and political perspectives.[2] The term 'studies' is deemed more appropriate than 'articles', 'essays' or 'theses' because the nature of their content is intendedly non-academic and aimed at a general audience, while the conversational and often allegorical mode of writing makes a direct appeal to the reader's own intuitive reasoning. As further explained below, the present study on *Heralding Article 25* forms a key component of Mesbahi's continuing works, and is therefore the first to be published in book form.

Because many readers might find the tenor and energy of this book to be unfamiliar, you are encouraged to adopt an open and engaged mindset that is unlike the usual mode of studying commentaries on social change. As Mesbahi asserts from the first page, world problems are now so complex in their totality that we have to look at political issues with 'a different kind of energy and perception' and with 'an attitude of renewed attention' if we want to perceive for ourselves their profounder meaning. This requires not just the retention of more facts and information, but what Mesbahi describes as an 'inward learning' that compels us to look within ourselves for new insight and understanding as we reflect on the problems of humanity. We don't need to look outwardly towards the author (or anyone else) to give us all the answers, as we can also seek inner confirmation about the spiritual and psychological reality of our interconnected lives—a reality that is generally obscured by social conditioning, ideological thinking and 'isms' in their many different forms.[3]

The author himself seeks to make clear that his writings are not based on scholarly research, but originate from his own inner investigations into the causes of, and solutions to, our converging global crises. As you will soon gather after reading this short book or any other of Mesbahi's studies, he reasons that those causes and solutions lie not within our current economic and political systems alone, which are the outer manifestation of a *spiritual* crisis that is at the root of world problems. And that spiritual crisis has resulted from the problem of human consciousness that stems back over the ages, reaching its climax in the present day through escalating conflicts, extreme global inequalities, worsening poverty amidst plenty, and environmental crises in all their dimensions. All of these outer crises are the consequence of humanity's longstanding failure to share (in a global and collective sense), which is a statement that may sound so simple to the educated mind that it is unlikely to make a meaningful impact. In consequence, Mesbahi's numerous studies aim to investigate and elucidate the significance of this premise from every possible angle, particularly in relation to the psychological factors that inhibit our perception of the need to share the world's resources as an international emergency.

To summarise an essential message from Mesbahi's work, global economic change for a better world is impossible without inner, transformational change within the individual on a collective and mass scale. Clearly, this psychological transformation of our conscious awareness cannot be brought about by merely reading intellectual analyses that endlessly dissect and debate the complexities of world problems. Much more is required of the engaged citizen at this time of unprecedented planetary upheaval, and it is in this light that Mesbahi's studies are best approached—as a joint investigation into the path of exit from today's culminating civilisational/spiritual crisis.

The specific line of enquiry pursued in this study is therefore concerned with how to bring about a worldwide awakening of compassion and empathy towards the poorest members of the human family, millions of whom are needlessly dying as each year passes. From the opening paragraph in chapter one, this essential theme is introduced in the simplest terms: that securing an adequate standard of living for all people is the first pivotal step towards realising a just, sustainable and peaceful future world. After a sweeping examination of the forces that stand in the way of achieving this ever viable objective, chapter two explores the wider political and economic implications of enabling every person on earth to live in dignity with the basics guaranteed. These implications extend to the issues of global conflict and environmental sustainability, the last of which is considered in greater detail in chapter three. In chapters four and five, the need to end hunger and life-threatening poverty as an incomparable global priority is further explored from various perspectives, with an emphasis on the shift in consciousness that is required for millions of people worldwide to gather in peaceful protest on behalf of this single aim.

While some of the political issues discussed may initially seem too specialist or academic for the general reader, it is hoped that the main subject of this book will soon be recognised as one of utmost importance to every person of goodwill in the crucial period ahead. That subject concerns not only the practical implementation of *Article 25* of the *Universal Declaration of Human Rights*; more significantly, the foremost question is what actions will be required from the global public to bring about this momentous turnaround in governmental priorities. Mesbahi thoroughly examines this question over the next five chapters, making it clear that the purpose of his enquiry with the reader is to try and reach a common understanding of 'the people's strategy' for world transformation.

There can be no hope of shifting governmental priorities in favour of the poorer two-thirds of the global population, he writes, without 'immense and unceasing civic engagement from the more privileged one-third of humanity'. Thus what can galvanise such a huge, united voice of ordinary citizens the world over? What is preventing this massive public engagement of people everywhere from taking place? And what can overcome the complacency and indifference that is so prevalent within modern affluent society, whereby the average person continues to remain oblivious while thousands of people die from easily preventable causes each day?

In the end, these sorts of questions cannot be answered through a conventional analysis of global issues followed by a precise conclusion or list of policy recommendations. It may be true that Mesbahi clearly offers one core proposal in this book, which is for enormous, continuous and worldwide protests that revolve around a united demand for governments to guarantee the human rights enshrined in *Article 25*. But no straightforward answer can be given for *how* to initiate these unparalleled demonstrations that require 'millions of people in each capital city congregated in unison, day after day and week after week in ever renewing numbers'. Therefore we as the reader (or 'joint investigator') are invited to ponder these questions for ourselves, and finally reach our own conclusions as to what specific actions we—as individuals or groups—should personally make to help achieve this overarching vision.

***

One aspect of Mesbahi's writings that will soon become apparent is his fusing of a spiritual perspective with contemporary political matters, which should not be misinterpreted as being of a faith-based or strictly religious point of view. Any reader of any religious or agnostic persuasion should be able to resonate with the integral observations that Mesbahi advances, provided we are able to maintain an open mind that examines world problems with a 'different kind of energy and perception' in accordance with the spirit and vision of his dialogue.

The perspective that Mesbahi invariably takes is from an understanding of the whole to the particular, while constantly emphasising the interrelatedness of world problems that arise from the aforementioned problem of human consciousness. Again and again, the reader is urged to look at global crises from a truly planetary, inclusive and holistic viewpoint, and with an awareness of 'our spiritual unity and interconnectedness'. This doesn't mean that we have to embrace any so-called New Age teachings about higher planes of existence or mysterious cosmic entities. On the contrary, the spiritual awareness that Mesbahi seeks to inculcate in the reader is concerned with seeing humanity as, in his words, 'one interdependent family in which everyone's needs are basically the same wherever we live in the world or whatever language we speak, and however seemingly different our outer forms of social organisation'.

From this distinctly human and earthly vantage, the spiritual themes that are addressed have potentially dramatic implications for our present social, economic and political structures. For example, the principle of right human relations is repeatedly mentioned throughout the chapters in a way that may lead us to reflect anew on this ageless concept, especially in the context of vast inequalities between the richest and poorest nations which are now being highlighted by uncontrollable migration patterns. Similarly, Mesbahi discusses the concept of goodwill in a way that gives us reason to think again about its meaning and relevance to the critical world situation, both in personal and global terms. The idea of the 'One Humanity' is also variously mentioned in contexts that again urge us to adopt a perspective of the whole to the particular, and consequently to perceive the urgency of implementing the principle of sharing into world affairs. Another key spiritual theme that Mesbahi focuses on, especially in chapter five, is the need for 'Self-knowledge' that is inhibited by our inadequate modes of education and the malign influence of rampant commercialisation in modern societies. When spelled with a capital 'S' to denote the higher form of knowing or awareness that Mesbahi is referring to, Self-knowledge in this sense clearly has spiritual connotations about our true nature as human beings and the higher meaning and purpose of our lives.

The instructions and guidance contained within these pages is therefore of a different order, and can only be grasped if the reader begins to think in terms of 'common sense through an engaged heart, and not on the basis of isms'—which is also a main topic of discussion in the fourth and fifth chapters. When approached in such a manner, Mesbahi's work can be regarded as a unique form of teaching that encourages us to grow in inner awareness about the spiritual/psychological reality of humanity's problems; to think for ourselves about the need for a transformation in human consciousness (both in individual and societal terms); and to connect with our intuitional mind as well as the lower intellect in trying to understand these imperative questions. The frequent use of analogies and metaphors can be appreciated in this vein, as can the various repetitions of certain themes that are intended to bring illumination from many angles, while constantly provoking the reader to think intuitively for themselves with compassion and inner awareness.

This may also help to explain why Mesbahi has striven to keep the language simple and accessible, without focusing on the technical details of what economic sharing means in policy terms. Although the second chapter does explore the broader political implications of implementing *Article 25*, this is always in principled terms and from a holistic or spiritual perspective that calls upon the reader themselves to discern the wider significances. Thus it becomes possible for us to have a relationship with the book as if we are reading our own thoughts and insights, however muted they may be within the hidden recesses of our hearts and minds. Then the book becomes not the mere personal opinions of an unconventional writer, but simple statements of truth about our combined potential to transform the world through the unbelievable power of massed goodwill. By reading and re-reading the manifest wisdom of the author's perceptions along these lines, we will hopefully be moved to live the words and put them into practice through our own actions.

If the teachings and guidelines contained within this book are taken seriously by enough people and subsequently acted upon, it may represent an entirely new chapter in the history of political activism. As some readers have already remarked about *Heralding Article 25* and Mesbahi's other studies, they constitute an effective roadmap for realising the better world that progressive thinkers of every stripe have long been striving towards. The fourth chapter on 'engaging the heart' is perhaps the clearest exposition written anywhere of what is needed to unite millions of ordinary citizens around the world through the simple cause of sharing global resources to irrevocably end poverty. This centres on a set of instructions for activists (and particularly the youth) to not fight 'against' the system or capitalism *per se*, but instead to 'be pragmatic by heralding one demand that can transcend our political differences in the most inclusive way'. A key element of Mesbahi's 'strategy for world transformation' thereby involves a new education that can equip citizens of every nation to think in terms of the 'One Humanity', beginning with a universal understanding of 'how the principles of sharing and cooperation are the foundation of a sustainable global economic system'. This essential theme—which is also the focus of our work at STWR—is explored in more detail in the last chapter through a challenging discussion on the true meaning of leadership, democracy, and freedom.

Of the many memorable observations that Mesbahi has informally raised in discussions at STWR, it is apt to repeat that there cannot be 'a' single solution to the challenges that face humanity in the twenty-first century. But we can be sure there exists a correct way of reaching the manifold solutions we need, regardless of the complexity of the world's crises among more than seven billion people. Such is the major enquiry that comprises the following pages, all of which revolve around the need for a united people's voice that is powerful enough to reorder governmental priorities. Through his compelling and provocative argumentation, Mesbahi invites us to contemplate the necessity of co-creating such a peaceful and implacable phenomenon, what he describes as a 'crucial and absent protagonist on the world stage—namely, the benevolent and all-embracing influence of educated public opinion on behalf of the unmet needs of the world's majority poor'. Whether this new superpower in global affairs fast emerges is a question that only we, ourselves, can ultimately answer.

Adam W. Parsons
Editor, Share The World's Resources

PART I

The failure of governments

"Everyone has the right to a standard of living adequate for the health and well-being of himself and of his family, including food, clothing, housing and medical care and necessary social services, and the right to security in the event of unemployment, sickness, disability, widowhood, old age or other lack of livelihood in circumstances beyond his control."

– UDHR, ARTICLE 25.1

One of the greatest hopes for humanity today lies in realising *Article 25* of the *Universal Declaration of Human Rights* for every man, woman and child across the world, since these modest provisions hold the key to resolving so many of our intractable problems. As repeatedly asserted in this series of studies,[4] it is imperative that *Article 25* becomes a foundational law and guiding principle within each country, which is far from the current reality in both the richest and poorest nations. The youth in particular are encouraged to adopt *Article 25* as their protest slogan, goal and vision, for its basic requirements have undreamt of implications for the future direction of international relations and global development. Now is the time for huge, continuous and worldwide demonstrations that uphold the long-agreed rights of *Article 25*—for adequate food, housing, healthcare and social security for all—until governments reorder their distorted priorities and finally implement the principle of sharing into world affairs.

In our highly complex and intellectualised societies, however, such a simple instruction is liable to be met with a litany of cross-questions and objections. For this reason it is necessary to examine from many angles the potential of *Article 25* to light the path towards a just, sustainable and peaceful world based on right human relations. If the solution to humanity's problems is indeed so simple and yet the problems themselves are so entrenched and complicated, then we clearly have to look at these issues afresh and with a different kind of energy and perception. The human mind has been heavily conditioned and misled through past wrong educational methods, hence to perceive the truth in its simplicity requires us to be inwardly free and detached—or at the least, free from the 'isms' and divisive ideologies that continue to suppress our common sense and innate spiritual intelligence.[5]

With such an attitude of renewed attention, let us therefore try to investigate the implications of fully realising the universal rights set out in *Article 25* as a foremost priority of the world's governments. What will be the effects of ending poverty and ensuring an adequate standard of living for the entire human population, not only socially, economically and politically, but also in terms of humanity's growth and spiritual evolution? How will prioritising *Article 25* lead to solutions for all the world's interlocking crises, including environmental degradation and global conflict? And hence why should ordinary people gather in their millions to uphold these fundamental rights, day after day in peaceful protest until governments decidedly act on a scale that is commensurate with human need? In short, why should we change our tactics by advocating for *Article 25* as

4

a universal strategy for world transformation, knowing that all the answers for saving our planet will mushroom out of this most basic set of demands?

Before we can examine these critical questions we are first compelled to acknowledge why our governments have failed to guarantee the full realisation of socio-economic human rights in every country, leaving literally billions of people without sufficient access to the necessities of life. There is no doubt that governments could ensure that everyone has access to an adequate standard of living, given the vast amount of wealth and resources that are available in the world. It is also true that the human rights encapsulated in *Article 25* have already been realised to a considerable degree in many affluent countries during the twentieth century, as best exemplified in the various welfare states of Scandinavian and other high-income countries. Yet such entitlements have hardly ever existed for a majority of the population in poorer countries, even as the prior social protection guarantees are being reneged upon or slowly dismantled in many of the most developed nations.

An extensive literature examines the complex reasons for this state of affairs, although the immediate cause could be understood rather bluntly: for most countries have a president or prime minister whose mission in office is not to prioritise the basic needs of all people, but rather to sign more contracts for big corporations and give the highest precedence to growing the economy. We can consider these leaders to be 'politico-accountants', concerned above all with profit for the nation and commercial opportunities through globalised trade and finance, while holding on to power at all costs instead of cooperating with other parties to render 'the equal and inalienable rights of all members of the human family' into a shared reality.

To look at world problems as broadly and candidly as possible, we may therefore observe that one of the biggest obstacles to securing *Article 25* for all people is the misguided priorities of our governments and the harmful practices of ruthlessly profit-driven business activity. Countless civil society reports and books are written that catalogue the indifference of multinational corporations with respect to the human rights of extremely poor or underprivileged citizens, in which these global money-making entities have developed expert proficiency in what may be called 'theft and destruction within the law'. This may entail appropriating the land and other vital resources that belong to the people of a nation, for example, or exploiting workers and depriving them of a living wage, or simply avoiding paying their due share of taxes to public coffers.

And in such a world where giant corporations are more powerful than many governments, our political representatives have no time for *Article 25* when thousands of their business contracts are potentially at stake. To be sure, the true advisor of world leaders today is not *Article 25* with its straightforward guidelines, but rather the forces of commercialisation that increasingly dictate every governmental policy in whichever country we may consider.[6] Even if a government or politician attempts to serve the common good of all people and the whole nation, it will not be long before powerful corporate lobby groups and financial interests push them in the opposite direction. And in that process of a well-meaning politician trying to change the world, no doubt the world will soon change them—through the sheer power of a malefic system that is based on the old ways of profit, privilege and competitive self-interest.

The distorted priorities of our governments are most visible on the international level, where foreign policies are fundamentally driven by the aggressive pursuit of hegemonic goals and economic dominance, and least of all by the prerogatives of *Article 25*. Trade between nations remains ever predicated on the urge of stronger nations to dominate the weaker, which in turn is coordinated by the geopolitical strategies of those rich countries that largely determine the trajectory of world affairs. If we could follow the movement of all the millions of lucrative business contracts around the world, we could perceive the source of all the major tensions and conflicts that continue to define the international picture. One nation wants a piece of cake in Africa, another wants its stake in South America, another vies for its claim on the energy assets located somewhere in Asia or the Middle East, and so on—all the time sowing seeds of distrust among the competing governments and fomenting global warfare. Thus the arrogance and duplicity of foreign policy in which powerful nations profess their high-minded values as enshrined in constitutional and international laws, and then proceed to exploit and grab from other countries instead of truly giving, aiding and serving on behalf of the good of all.

Since the inauguration of the United Nations there is a clear link between the non-realisation of *Article 25* and American foreign policy specifically, for it is the domineering and self-seeking ambitions of America that have led to so many wars and so much destruction throughout the world, as ever supported by its subservient allies and followers. The global stratagems and covert manoeuvrings of the Pentagon, the C.I.A. and other U.S. intelligence agencies are effectively a case study in the indirect denial of *Article 25* in many of the most impoverished or conflict-ridden nations. Yet world politics in its entirety is like a field of boundless research into the incidental creation of poverty, which is generally hidden behind supposedly righteous pretexts such as the national interest or state security. Even the phrase 'foreign policy' connotes division and injustice in a world of excessive wealth inequalities, and represents the antithesis of right human relations—no matter what is deviously stated in official documentation and policy rhetoric. Indeed in such an unequal world that is brazenly governed by the principle of self-interest, not a single foreign policy is based on right relationship between the peoples of different nations or their representative governments.

We are therefore credulous if we believe our governments when they profess to be concerned with eliminating poverty and securing the human rights of *Article 25*, when the only way they can remain in power is by prioritising large corporate and influential private interests, both domestically and abroad. It's actually a hypocrisy if an international conference is convened by heads of state to professedly end the existence of needless human deprivation, while these same governments continue to sign contracts for multinational corporations to appropriate land, extract natural resources and privatise essential public services in foreign countries, often with devastating consequences for the very poorest people and communities. It may be a decent and moral ambition to completely eradicate so-called 'extreme' poverty by 2030, as enshrined in the latest commitments for the Sustainable Development Goals, but it is not the first time that world leaders have made such vain promises to uplift the poorest of the poor. With the best intentions of bureaucrats and policymakers, it will still remain impossible that any such aspiration can be achieved within the context of the 'commercialisation paradigm', to coin an appropriate term.

There is only one route to end poverty and bring balance to this earth, irrespective of how long humanity has ignored this perennial obligation: to cooperatively organise the global economy in order to share the resources of the world, and thence redistribute wealth to where it rightfully belongs. Considering the overwhelming scale of severe poverty that persists within our fast growing human population, there can be no true expression of world goodwill without a massive redistribution of resources to the most disadvantaged and beleaguered countries, based on these two principles that merit constant repeating: that is, economic sharing and (as yet hardly witnessed) genuine international cooperation.

As each critical year passes by, how many millions of people will have died from preventable poverty-related causes, whether or not we experience another global financial crisis? And what will it take for the world's richest governments to share their surplus food and other material goods with the millions of impoverished people in dire need of immediate help and sustenance? Such an accomplishment would necessarily involve diverting considerable amounts of additional finances to underfunded humanitarian agencies, and even the use of military personnel and equipment that is always on hand for 'other' purposes. It could certainly be

9

achieved with a mere fraction of the money and resources that is always at the disposal of governments, corporations, wealthy individuals and private institutions.

But until the common sense of sharing governs economic relationships, may God help any person who lives in a vast slum or poor village with nine children who they can't adequately provide for, and don't count on any government pledges or development goals to prevent any such family from falling into complete destitution. Hence *Article 25* is the big thorn that politicians will find in their sides during any international conference about eradicating global poverty, and we can expect more of the same conferences every ten or fifteen years so long as they continue to follow the prevailing paradigm of commercialisation—if only humanity can survive in the meantime.

Furthermore, we are fooling ourselves as much as the poor if we believe that our governments can succeed in tackling the root causes of hunger and poverty, so long as the mindset of charity pervades in our society and culture. What is charity, in truth, if not the result of the State manipulating the benevolence of its own people, while leaving the least privileged among us to fight just to feed and sustain themselves on this bounteous planet? From the most holistic perspective, we can observe how the very existence of charity is undignifying in a world of material and financial abundance, when today everyone could easily be granted the means to guarantee that their health and wellbeing is adequately provided for. Arguably, it is our government's historical indifference to poor people's economic insecurity that has given rise to the existence of charity over the course of many centuries, in which sense charity *per se* is borne out of social injustice and not true sharing, solidarity or love. We might wonder if the practise of charity would ever have come into existence if the human rights outlined in *Article 25* had already been established in every country of the world many thousands of years ago.

Yet despite all of humanity's progress in science and technology, the only established international system we have in place to embody right human relations is voluntary donations of overseas 'development assistance', which has always been debased through self-interest and profit-making to a significant degree, as long recognised by civil society organisations. In a similar vein, we can also observe how the very idea of giving 'humanitarian aid' is an affront to our commonality as a family of nations, when those surpluses of food and other resources should not have been accumulated by rich countries in the first place, but rightfully shared all along. From a planetary viewpoint it may make sense to talk of humanitarian aid if people from Mars or Venus were helping us here on Earth, but humanity is one interdependent family that has always been bestowed with the produce and capacity to ensure that everyone's needs are unconditionally (and forever) met. Would we describe our actions as humanitarian aid if our own children were dying from hunger, God forbid, and we shared with them a meagre amount of the provisions that we casually enjoy each day, thereafter proudly hailing ourselves as a good philanthropist? Or would we unreservedly and urgently help them as a humble act of love, caring only for their life and welfare without any thought that we are being charitable?

To look at this question with awareness and compassion reveals how the very term 'humanitarian aid' is psychologically

11

meaningless and absurd, and it tells us everything we need to know about how humanity has become so divided and corrupt. How arrogant and degrading to use such phraseology as 'U.S. Aid' on freights of surplus produce that are transported to destitute people abroad, among the rife injustice and institutionalised thievery that maintains the stark discrepancies in living standards between rich and poor countries. We have noted before how such wealthy nations first accumulate their surplus produce through unjust economic practices that routinely exploit the labour and natural resources of less developed countries, before they redistribute a tiny proportion of these ill-gotten gains to help alleviate the poverty that they also cause—and then they call that humanitarian aid.[7] Can we thus perceive how the mainstream conception of aid is contrary to the real meaning of goodwill and humility, especially when governments have long agreed that the necessities of life should be made accessible for the benefit of all (as indeed spelled out in *Article 25*)? Like the word charity, such a phrase would never have come into being if our societies were based on common sense and right human relationship from the start, for there is no such thing as 'humanitarian aid' from within the psychological awareness of love.

We may well have accepted this terminology of aid without contemplating its significance because we are habituated to leave such issues to politicians, expecting them to do everything for us. But if we can perceive the duplicity of our governments who profess to be concerned with ending poverty while continuing to exploit the poorest people and countries, maybe it's time for us to wake up and ask them: where's the missing part? Where's the love, the kindness, the common sense of preventing people from dying of hunger in a world of plenty? Perhaps we should all crowd into those government summits and conclaves about eradicating poverty, and together ask our political representatives: 'If you really care about helping the poor then why don't you share the world's resources more equally among all nations, instead of making non-binding development goals and merely redistributing insufficient amounts of foreign aid?'

And if we as ordinary people are truly concerned about ending the injustice of hunger so that it never happens again, then maybe we should apply the same question to ourselves: where's the missing part? Where's the caring, the compassion, the concern for defending the basic rights of those who live in a continual state of want and penury? Is it enough to press our politicians to send more aid to poor countries on our behalf, or does the love we have for our fellow human beings compel us to go before the government and say: 'This shameful situation cannot continue—it's time to save our starving brothers and sisters as your utmost collective priority!' What kind of education and conditioning has led us to accept this state of affairs, and what's to stop us demanding from the governments of the world: WHERE'S THE MISSING PART?

As a consequence of our engrained and debasing attitudes towards charity and overseas aid, those charities that are seriously engaged with ameliorating social problems and helping the poor are themselves forced to become politicised, and thereby oppose the government policies and corporate activity that is further perpetuating the causes of poverty. Otherwise, the more energy that is given to charity by well-meaning groups and citizens, the more governments can continue to pursue their distorted and harmful priorities, such as by building up more armaments for war instead of feeding the hungry as a matter of emergency.

None of this is meant to question the venerable necessity of charity which, as this writer has repeatedly acknowledged, is largely and thankfully a force for good in our grotesquely unequal social order.[8] Rather, we are trying to holistically observe the absurdity of our governments pledging to end poverty at some later date—through charitable means and *not* true sharing or justice—in a world that has more than enough resources available for everyone, even with the burgeoning population levels of the present day. Hopefully in generations to come we'll look back at history and perceive the existence of charity in the twenty-first century for what it really is, which is the inevitable and ultimately unnecessary by-product of political indifference and public complacency.

***

In our dysfunctional societies with their confused and morally bankrupt politicians, it is instructive to ponder on the relationship that exists between the meaning of prosperity, economic growth and *Article 25*. What does it mean to prosper in a world where you have many nations with large numbers of their population living in unbearable poverty, amidst a minority of nations that are relatively wealthy and privileged in their lifestyles?

Imagine there is a town where everyone is so 'prosperous' that they leave surplus foodstuffs rotting in huge storehouses and costly waste products scattered in rubbish dumps, yet a neighbouring town is so poor that they do not even have enough resources to ensure the right of everyone to a standard of living adequate for health and wellbeing, as stipulated in *Article 25*. Does it make any sense for the mayor of the wealthy town to proudly hail their high level of economic growth and prosperity, regardless of the indigence and misery that is lurking over the horizon? If the mayor does not decide to share the town's resources with their neighbour, sooner or later the neighbouring town will come to them in one way or another—even the cats and dogs of the poverty-stricken town will try to eat in the other one by any means necessary. Notwithstanding the oversimplification of applying such an analogy to the world situation, is this so dissimilar to how different countries relate to each other on an international or regional basis, where the most affluent nations live with relative indifference to the deprivation experienced by the majority poor overseas?

Hence we should be psychologically aware of these misleading, ugly and vulgar terms 'prosperity' and 'economic growth' that are so often repeated by politicians and economists on our television screens. In this unfortunate world where levels of population growth and poverty are rapidly rising, where the environment is being continuously ravaged and despoiled, where climate change is already causing havoc and ruin for millions of poor families, how can prosperity be anything other than precarious and lead to anything but disorder—that is, unless that prosperity is equitably shared across the world? How can these terms be anything but ugly, vulgar and even stupid in the present-day reality of extreme global inequality, and how can they make any moral sense in a world that allows millions of people to die from needless poverty, and denies many millions of others from having enough nutritious food to eat, or clean water or adequate shelter, or even the most basic form of healthcare to keep them alive and well?

Our political leaders may well profess that they want every citizen within their nation to thrive and prosper, but how can that prosperity be achieved within one nation alone when the world is infected with a deadly virus—one that is not called Ebola, but rather the forces of commercialisation? A rampant plague in our societies that not only conditions you to become prosperous at the expense of others, but also influences you to think that you're better than those less fortunate than yourself until you, too, are part of humanity's collective arrogance and indifference. What we call 'the system' is now so deeply characterised by the selfish pursuit of wealth and success that it is even creating a new wave of thought, which can be crudely précised as hatred of the poor in one's own country as well as the people of other nations who are less privileged than oneself.

The quest for endless economic growth is therefore dangerous in our confused and fragmented societies that are almost entirely overshadowed by the forces of commercialisation, in which context such growth can only lead to further division, disorder, sorrow and ultimately violence. Underneath all the deceitful propaganda and mind conditioning of modern times, the myopic pursuit of economic growth signifies a growing separation between citizens and the state, and really means 'let's enable the rich to grow even richer and create more billionaires in the midst of the poor'. Economic growth in these circumstances is tantamount to private accountancy for large corporations, and its meaning has become as absurd from a psychological perspective as the concept of charity in a world of plenty.

Hence it is a grave mistake for politicians to keep using this phraseology that connotes 'commercialisation growth' and not the growth of a healthy, just or sustainable economy. What is that economic growth for, in a society that is becoming increasingly inequitable and divided? Even in the recent past when many nations didn't have the same levels of debt as today, there was still widespread poverty and hunger in the rich world as well as the poor. So we should ask our political representatives: economic growth for what purpose, and for whose benefit? For the sake of a system that has caused immense suffering and chaos, and is now rapidly melting from within?

No politician can talk meaningfully about economic growth while allowing the forces of commercialisation to take over their agenda. A statesman or stateswoman with the most inclusive and honourable intention will still incite danger and eventual disaster by promoting further growth of the present system, regardless of whether their short-sighted purpose is to 'create more jobs'. Again we should ask our political representatives: jobs for what purpose, and for whose benefit? For the purpose of building mega-casinos, private shopping malls, luxury apartments and more armaments factories in the middle of a spiritually, morally and economically broken population, and for the benefit of millionaires who pay their disposable workers the minimum wage according to the law?

Only through new economic arrangements based on the principle of sharing can we talk with any meaning about growing the economy and creating decent employment, although then our focus will have to enlarge beyond our solely national concerns to encompass the needs of the world as a whole. And that will immediately obligate our political representatives to administer a reformed system of global governance that can ensure a more equitable distribution of resources between all countries, with a reversal in governmental priorities towards immediately securing the urgent needs of the very poor, beginning with those who are deprived of sufficient food and other essential resources necessary for their survival.

If the government of any nation is truly concerned about meeting the needs of all its citizens, perhaps then it can talk with sagacity about economic growth, so long as it speaks through *Article 25* as its bible. For in that instance, the government will have to restructure the economy to ensure that wealth, resources and economic opportunities are fairly shared among the population. And the precondition for ensuring a just distribution of resources is to remove the claws of commercialisation from every aspect of society, and to reorient the government's spending priorities away from armaments and other harmful corporate subsidies. At the same time, no longer can each society continue to degrade the environment through conspicuous and wasteful consumption, if the guiding principle of economic activity is to ensure that everyone has what they need for a dignified life in perpetuity. Any sane politician must now agree that this is a self-evident supposition when the economy can only be sustained within a biosphere that is healthy and self-renewing, and no longer strained beyond all limits of endurance.

But even if a more enlightened nation enshrines *Article*

25 into law and commits itself to a sustainable, fair and balanced distribution of resources among its own population, their contentment and prosperity will be short-lived if they try to remain separated from the problems of other nations. To recall our analogy of the neighbouring prosperous and impoverished towns, it won't be long until the nation that rightly shares its domestic resources is besieged by the poor from distant places who try to enter into its borders—and by whatever means possible, whether or not there are punitive immigration controls and a state security apparatus in the way.

There can be no such thing as a healthy society in our divided and yet economically integrated world, where greed, selfishness and theft are driving forces behind financial and economic activity. If we suppose that only a single country implements *Article 25* to its fullest extent, while every other nation that has the means to do so instead follows the path of unbridled commercialisation, then it doesn't mean that there is something wrong with every country *except for* the one that collectively pools and shares its wealth. It means there is something wrong with the whole of humanity, because humanity is one in its nature, or one in the eyes of what we might term 'Life' or 'God'. We are one human family within one spiritual evolution, which is not a strictly religious or 'New Age' observation but an eternal truth that is being gradually realised within numerous fields of scientific investigation. Every nation of the world is interconnected not just in a material or objective sense through global trade, travel and communication, but also energetically and subjectively in terms of the One Life that we share with every living being on Planet Earth, from the mineral kingdom to the non-physical and highest spiritual realms.

From this transcendent and revelatory understanding of our existence that can either be realised intuitively or recognised through a study of Ancient Wisdom teachings as well as Indigenous cosmologies, we can see how humanity is like a physical body that has to be cared for as a whole, without neglecting certain limbs or parts while only tending to others. If one side of the human body is functioning well but the other side is neglected and diseased, then the sickness will certainly affect the health and wellbeing of the entire person. Similarly, no single nation can remain separated from other nations however fairly and healthily they try to live, especially not in a world where commercialisation is intensifying with such speed that neither society nor the environment can withstand the strain for much longer.

Such is the paradox of policymaking in this era of planetary crisis and transition; no politician can afford the luxury of doing something good for his country in isolation, when that good has to be achieved in every other country simultaneously and absolutely. Hence no nation can make it alone, but all nations can make it together—through the principles of cooperation and sharing. We have no other exit strategy from the world's problems and hence it *must* be achieved with urgency whether our governments are ready or not, otherwise it may soon be the end of all of us. There cannot be one country out of more than 190 countries in this world that implements *Article 25* to the fullest extent, unless we decide to call that one country 'humanity', and ignore the rest. For there is only the One Humanity, indivisible from the whole.

What other reason need there be to share the resources of the world, and thus realise the fundamental rights of every man and woman—if not to allow the soul to carry out its life purpose within the individuality of its reflection? This is the deeper reality of our lives that ever was and forever will be, however much our understanding of world goodwill and right human relations has been corrupted by the melding of our self-centredness, ignorance and confusion over many lifetimes. If humanity is to become united as a reflection of who we are in our true spiritual nature, it is therefore imperative that activists, engaged citizens and our political representatives call for *Article 25* to be comprehensively guaranteed in every country of the world, and as a leading governmental priority for all nations. The time has come when we must not only raise our voices for the good of our own country, but also for the good of all the people of the world. The fortunate citizens who have their basic needs met already should sympathise with and join the many groups who do not, and thereby herald *Article 25* and the principle of sharing as our common cause.

Every person in North America, Western Europe, Australia and other affluent world regions should pause to ask themselves the question: what about the others who don't have access to the basic resources that I take for granted? These are the words that our politicians should also use about the millions of people living in poverty abroad, as well as within their own country's borders: what about the others? Then we will at least be inclined to share the surplus resources of our nation, and demand that our governments work with other nations to meet the enduring goal of *freedom from want* for everyone in the world. That is when a nation becomes an ally to *Article 25* and the principle of sharing, until eventually the very idea of an 'illegal immigrant' becomes contrary to anyone's understanding of how the world functions, along with any contemporary notion of 'charitable giving', 'humanitarian aid', 'foreign policy' or 'national self-interest'.

PART II

A brief rationale

Following the previous line of reasoning, we may easily perceive the many complex factors that prevent the full and permanent realisation of *Article 25* within all nations, from our government's misguided priorities to the sheer indifference of multinational corporations, the rapacity and inhumanness of foreign policy objectives, and ingrained attitudes of charity in place of justice. We may also begin to perceive the unimagined outcomes of ensuring that basic needs are secured for every man, woman and child without exception, which is necessary to reflect upon in order to understand intellectually the many reasons why heralding *Article 25* is a viable strategy for world rescue and rehabilitation.

As already emphasised, the requisite money and resources have long been available to guarantee all people's socio-economic human rights, and within a relatively short space of time if every government—working through the United Nations and its relevant agencies—coalesced in their efforts to urgently stop the moral outrage of preventable poverty-related fatalities. But the policies of even the richest countries only minimally reflect the needs of the relative poor within their own borders, and far less do they serve the interests of the most excluded and disregarded poor people in other nations, resulting in a huge avoidable death toll as each day passes.

How extraordinary it is that world leaders can come together and produce allies to go to war within a matter of weeks, and yet they can never produce enough allies to come to the aid of the world's hungry and impoverished. The only adequate international response we have seen to alleviate this intolerable situation was expressed in the Brandt Commission Report of 1980, which proposed an emergency programme of economic sharing to end hunger and absolute poverty once and for all—but now lies buried and forgotten in the archives of history.[9]

After so many years of political inaction only the massed goodwill of ordinary people can bring morality and sanity to global affairs, and influence a re-ordering of government priorities through enormous and continual public protests within all countries. Only the world's people united can impel nations to cooperate in implementing *Article 25*, and perhaps only then will we see the right politicians come to the fore who will summon the necessary allies and military resources for saving lives on a tremendous scale, rather than further compromising those lives or taking them away. Perhaps then will we see the immense public engagement that every progressive activist is after, until no political leader can remain in office without following the benevolent concerns of those ordinary citizens who elected them to power.

Through such an unprecedented worldwide outpouring of compassion for the least fortunate among us, perhaps then there will be no role for the politico-accountant who is only interested in keeping their prestigious job, playing at being the powerful diplomat with an expensive suit and tie.

Let's not forget that we are here considering the injustice of poverty that is happening across the world in its entirety, and that does not mean a small number of people dying from hunger in the least developed countries each week; it means at least 40,000 people dying from poverty-related causes every day, many of which occur in middle-income countries and are known to be largely preventable.[10] How much longer do we want to witness the recurring spectacle of these global conferences on tackling poverty and hunger, while nothing is done on an adequate scale to help these tragically neglected people? Is it not true that all the millions of dollars spent on organising such high-level summits over several decades could instead have been used to save many lives already? Meanwhile, we—the minority privileged who take the human rights of *Article 25* for granted—continue to overconsume and waste the world's food and other essential commodities, instead of demanding that our governments redistribute our nation's surplus resources to where they are most critically needed. How many more Brandt Reports do we need to shake our conscience about this ongoing atrocity that apparently warrants so little of our attention?

***

Now let us try to put aside our objections and imagine that our governments are seriously compelled by the people's will to implement *Article 25*, and then consider the dramatic implications of achieving this assuredly attainable goal. Obviously it is unviable for everyone to live in dignity with the basics guaranteed unless the economy is structured in such a way that essential resources are more equally distributed, and essential public services are made accessible to all. But such a commonsensical understanding is incompatible with the market forces ideology that has come to dominate mainstream political thinking, leading to the creation of laws and institutions that further private interests and the profit-making potential of large corporations.

What, then, would be the consequences for these corporatised rules and institutions that underpin society if guaranteeing *Article 25* becomes the foremost governmental priority for every nation? Undoubtedly, the effect would be socially, economically and politically transformative, especially when we consider what we know about the forces of commercialisation: that *Article 25* counts for almost nothing in their wake. For example, no longer could corporations be permitted to wantonly grab land, speculate on food, and hoard or destroy their surplus produce whilst people are dying of hunger in the world. And no longer could politicians prioritise economic growth and corporate profits through the commercialisation of public services, if they are really concerned with meeting all people's needs through a systematised sharing of the nation's resources. After a certain time, many complex laws that exclusively promote profit-making interests would have to be reversed or significantly reformed, and new ones created that are truly moral and fair, thus enabling human goodwill to flourish in world affairs.

Indeed if the primary consideration behind any state

law or policy is to safeguard the human rights of *Article 25*, then it would soon become apparent that existing global trade agreements are inherently biased and unjust. This can be understood very simply, for if I imagine that I am the president of a poor country that has established *Article 25* as a foundational law that informs all government decisions, then that law would tell me to make sure that every family is well fed and cared for before I look to do anything else. In which case, I cannot allow my poorest farmers and labourers to be exploited by exporting their goods for a cheap price, only for the benefit of wealthy consumers in distant cities and overseas countries—I will have to demand that the trade rules are changed so that the farmers can feed themselves and their own community first. And the multinational corporations who dictate the terms of unfair trade can do nothing to stop me if *Article 25* is the law for every country and the guiding light for global policy, supervised by the United Nations with the worldwide backing of public opinion.

From every angle, the implications are all-encompassing once the overriding influence of profit, greed and unbridled market forces is held in check through appropriate state interventions and regulations. The relentless corporate lobbying and drive to make money from legitimated theft will inevitably be compromised and progressively weakened, hence implementing *Article 25* is effectively one of the worst enemies that ruthlessly profit-driven corporations can face. As business activity starts to take a different route through the guidance of economic policies that are predicated on the principle of sharing, perhaps it will not be long before the endemic corruption that blights every government—in both rich and poor countries to different degrees—also gradually diminishes over time. What incentive would there be for those who are greedy for power to enter the political domain if national governance truly serves the common good, as of course it should do instead of primarily functioning on behalf of global corporations and wealthy individuals?

Try to visualise the effect of governments around the world acting to safeguard the human rights of *Article 25* due to the irresistible pressure from enormous, continuous and implacable street demonstrations in each country. While the poorest people of less developed nations will joyously welcome this awakening of public awareness towards their plight, the first effect of redistributing global resources to help them may be to bring government corruption to its most visible height. So long as this corruption persists and oppressive politicians misuse the aid they receive on behalf of their populations, there will definitely be an uprising of ordinary citizens until the party responsible is removed from office and replaced. And if a dictatorial leadership still holds on to power through violence and state repression, why can't representatives from the United Nations be sent in to monitor their activities and gather any incriminating evidence? Just as the United Nations sends inspectors to monitor wars or search for nuclear weapons, is it not possible for an empowered United Nations agency to help ensure that any aid donated is used for its intended purposes?

We can further prophesise the consequences of implementing *Article 25* for those multilateral institutions that have long relinquished their duty to work on behalf of ordinary people and the poor. First and foremost, this would include the World Bank and International Monetary Fund that are so much maligned for imposing their egregious economic 'norms' on the rest of the world. In light of *Article 25* becoming the founding basis of a new global economic order, these organisations would either have to be decommissioned or wholly re-imagined to play a vital role in facilitating a process of massive resource redistribution, global governance restructuring and international economic reform—which altogether constitutes the first major step towards inaugurating a better world. After all, no institution is kept alive by itself but only by the people who sustain it, and we are here contemplating the onset of a more enlightened era of human civilisation that is characterised by an equal concern for the welfare of every person, not only the good of privileged affluent people or powerful self-serving nations.

In our divided world of today, the implementation of *Article 25* would clearly have an extraordinarily transformative effect on international relations and the foreign policies of major industrialised countries, which is an outcome that can again be considered from many angles and in simple terms. To begin with, a drastic reordering of global priorities towards meeting the basic needs of all people is evidently dependent on achieving a rapid de-escalation of military activity, alongside steep cuts in armaments budgets. This is not only essential for the United States which continues to dwarf the spending of all other countries, but also for those less developed nations with high incidences of poverty that are allocating increasing amounts to defence expenditures—often more than healthcare, education or social welfare.

Furthermore, we previously considered how world politics is broadly based on the opposite principles to economic sharing and genuine international cooperation, whilst the foreign policies of the United States and other G7 countries, in particular, are effectively telling the world that 'commercialisation is the right way for humanity to live'— leading to the increasing denial of *Article 25* in many less developed countries. The unsustainable trajectory of world affairs therefore compels us to envision what implementing this hallowed Article will mean for long-term relations between nation states. From the outset, America will have to stop playing the great imperial hegemon and finally utilise its ample resources to lead the way in eliminating worldwide poverty, instead of continuing in its arrogant pursuit of global power and domination. Russia will have to learn to live in peace as a true commonwealth of federated independent states, and concentrate on evolving together with greater regional autonomy instead of pursuing its military capability and coercive international influence. Likewise, China will have to stop building up its naval fleet and war machine as an insurance policy for its growing economic supremacy, and forego its land grabbing strategies by cooperating with other nations to share the resources of the world.

It may seem exceptionally idealistic to anticipate such a turnaround in economic and political relations among competing governments, but who cares to contemplate an alternative scenario in which the *modus operandi* of global affairs continues indefinitely into the future? The remorseless and mercenary foreign policies that are purportedly high-minded are gradually leading us towards a third world war in the near future—as a result of mounting extremes of inequality within and among countries, if not through intensified rivalry over increasingly scarce resources. Surely the more rational politicians and diplomats realise that the family of nations will soon be left with the ultimate choice: to cooperate and share in remedying these perilous conditions, or to slowly witness humanity's irreversible downfall.

We can further extrapolate for ourselves the many positive outcomes of implementing *Article 25* across the world, considering how nations will be led to restructure their economies and work in cooperation with other nations towards this mutual and imperative goal. When governments are duly obligated to ensure that every child and adult out of more than 7 billion people is well fed, healthy and materially secure (as well as guaranteed a free, quality public education as prescribed in Article 26), we may find that many other global problems are automatically solved along the way. This stands to reason, and can be deduced from the internationally coordinated measures that are patently necessary in this modern age of globalisation to guarantee the social and economic rights of all people.

Each nation would soon be compelled to make an inventory of the surplus resources they have at their disposal, including technology, knowledge, manpower and institutional capacity, as well as food, medicines, manufactured products, and any other basic materials or essential goods. A large-scale transfer of these resources to the poorest countries and regions would have to be organised through the United Nations and its global network of aid agencies, or through a new United Nations agency that is set up for the express purpose of overseeing a short-term emergency programme, which may have to continue apace for several years. Even North Korea may join in if the political will for such a programme presides among its neighbouring countries, whereby all people can be granted sufficient access to the world's essential resources through an unparalleled process of international redistribution.

Once the overriding objective of alleviating hunger and providing immediate relief to all those who live in conditions of absolute poverty has been achieved, comprehensive reform of the international political, economic and financial systems will assume a momentous importance in order to establish a more balanced and equal distribution of world resources among all countries. On a national level, much is already known and tested regarding the suitable arrangements needed to institute effective systems of redistribution in order to guarantee universal access to social protection and public services. In the same way, modern history in the post-war period attests to the various policies and regulations that can prohibit an ever-increasing concentration of wealth and power among a small minority of a country's population. As yet, however, few leading economists, financiers or politicians have contemplated the new institutional arrangements and economic practices that will be needed to establish a permanent system of resource sharing on a global basis. Therefore, if we can believe that world leaders will eventually see the necessity of reformulating the entire nature and purpose of development, we should expect an extensive process of research and dialogue before it is possible to realise the common ownership and cooperative management of the world's resources by the international community.

At the onset of this magnanimous endeavour, governments would do well to revisit and revise the recommendations in the Brandt Reports of 1980 and 1983. Although these policy documents may well be outdated after 35 years, they still contain an inspired outline of what it means to render the implementation of *Article 25* as a principal guide to political attitudes and global economic activity.[11] No doubt their proposals were constrained by the orthodox economic assumptions of their time, and hence they remain insufficient to deal with the extent of today's interlocking crises. But if the Cancun Summit had been taken seriously in 1981, then by now *Article 25* could have been well established as an effective set of laws within each nation that governs its society and the behaviour of political, economic and social institutions.[12]

In the event of such a transformation of government purposes across the world, the United Nations will have to be democratically reformed and re-empowered as the highest international authority in order to fulfil its original mandate. Without question, the epochal task of unifying global economic governance under a restructured United Nations system remains an outstanding requirement of the dawning twenty-first century. Whilst each country needs to implement the law of *Article 25* in its own way and according to the most appropriate methods, it will require the Assembly of Nations to oversee and enforce the tenets of those laws as an inviolable code for how all countries conduct their affairs on the global level.

By this means, the United Nations may truly live up to its name as a preeminent global institution that inherently calls upon member states to preserve peace, protect the vulnerable and promote cooperative international relations. If its various agencies are strengthened in order to play a major role in upholding the basic rights of *Article 25* for all people, then all of the other articles in the *Universal Declaration of Human Rights* may finally begin to fall into their right place. Thus in a figurative sense we may come to perceive *Article 25* as the supreme law of human dignity, and its implementation will mark the beginning of 'human rights' as a concept becoming proud of itself once again. Then the beauty and promise of the United Nation's founding vision may be recognised anew in the hearts and minds of ordinary people, with a reawakened understanding of its indispensable future potential.

However, this will have nothing to do with the Security Council and its unmerited functions and powers, which is a remnant of the old competitive and nationalistic ways of the past that are symbolised by the illusion 'I am still powerful and always will be'. When it comes to the self-interest of the major industrialised countries, only then do presidents and prime ministers defer to the United Nations and try to manipulate its system to their own ends. But when it comes to the interests of the public as a whole in every country, then it's as if the United Nation's obligations on member states no longer exist. The Security Council has no relation to the search for real international peace or security, as it rather functions like a private club whose members are represented by prominent politico-accountants, all of whom vote for or against its resolutions depending on how big is their prospective slice of the world's cake. And it is that constant vying for the lion's share of global resources that characterises the national security games of this outmoded Council, in contradistinction to the original purposes and principles of the United Nations as stated in the first chapter of its charter. The Security Council should never have been established to begin with, and should long ago have been dissolved to allow the General Assembly to take its place as a truly democratic global forum (with any rights to veto decisions abolished). In the meanwhile, the reality of war will continue to be sustained on the supposedly legitimate basis of power politics, national selfishness, and the exploitation of weaker populations in the pursuit of purely commercial or materialistic goals.

We can easily expand upon this line of reasoning to envision how a phenomenal public demand for implementing *Article 25* will eventually lead to global economic restructuring and genuine international cooperation, a significant lessening of the tension and conflict that characterises intergovernmental relations, and the eventual dissolution of the Security Council in line with the true destiny of the United Nations. What need will there be for a Security Council, in any case, if nations are cooperating in sharing the resources of the world and thus eliminating the economic roots of terrorism and conflict? Although let us be clear: this does not infer that the implementation of *Article 25* will in itself bring about a systemic alternative to globalised hyper-capitalism, and suddenly solve all of the world's problems at a stroke. There is no question that even if we were to rapidly meet the minimal needs enshrined in *Article 25* for all people, it would still not be sufficient to pose an effective challenge to prevailing power structures and undemocratic political regimes, or otherwise remedy the stark divisions in wealth and income between rich and poor countries.

Thus to query if securing the human rights of *Article*

25 is the only antidote for world problems is to pursue the wrong line of reasoning, as clearly a vast amount of further economic and political changes need to happen before we can foresee the fulfilment of all the United Nation's many noble aspirations. There is an interminable debate on the required means to achieve these ends, but the purpose of our enquiry is to try and reach a common understanding of the people's strategy for ushering in the necessary future transformations. As we have already established, there can be no hope of shifting governmental priorities in favour of the poorer two-thirds of the global population without immense and unceasing civic engagement from the more privileged one-third of humanity. Without this crucial and absent protagonist on the global stage—namely, the benevolent and all-embracing influence of educated public opinion on behalf of the unmet needs of the world's majority poor—then it is unfeasible that any structural blueprint for building a better world can come to fruition.

In this sense, the only alternative to the present socioeconomic order is to be found in a united voice of the people of goodwill throughout the world, and it is the widespread complacency of the average man and woman that gives us the impression that 'there is no alternative'. If we accept that the principle of sharing must underlie any global systemic alternative for a sustainable future, then *Article 25 reflects* that principle and *calls* for it to be implemented into world affairs. In truth there really is no alternative until an awareness of the urgency of ending extreme human deprivation is felt within every household, and nurtured in the hearts and minds of ordinary people as their most pressing concern.

Such is the quandary for the progressive thinkers who propose a new vision of society along with the policies needed to get there, because it will never happen unless the people of the world together embrace that vision and work for its fulfilment. As we will go on to explore in more detail, this alone explains why *Article 25* holds *within* itself the alternative that we are all looking for, and why its simple prescriptions can lead us to that alternative directly, naturally and seemingly miraculously. In due course, we may find that implementing *Article 25* is a direct gateway to manifold economic solutions and the surest path to freedom and justice, although its unknown potential will only come alive and reveal itself when humanity speaks the magic word. And the magic word is expressed through huge demonstrations in every country that are passionately focused on this end, and persist without interruption.

PART III

The environment question

PART II

The Implementation

One main objection that may arise in many people's minds concerns the question of environmental sustainability, and whether heralding *Article 25* as the people's principal cause is to disregard the urgency of ecological issues. This is another important matter to reflect upon as humanity now clearly faces two global emergencies of unprecedented magnitude: atmospheric pollution and environmental degradation, as well as hunger and increasing levels of poverty, inequality and social exclusion. So how can the implementation of *Article 25* pose a solution for all of these interlocking systemic crises?

In the first instance, an answer to this question can be understood logically and through simple deductive reasoning, even if such a conclusion is far from mainstream thinking at the present time. Here is the premise that we should consider for ourselves: that we can never tackle climate change or the environmental crisis without also remedying the injustice of poverty amidst plenty, which is where the solution to our manifold ecological problems initially begins. And this again should be contemplated from many angles, including psychological, moral and spiritual perspectives.

We have now discussed how an enormous groundswell of popular support for implementing Article 25 must immediately translate into drastic changes in government spending priorities, such as the reallocation of subsidies from armaments budgets to public service provision and social welfare within each country, alongside unrestricted aid for the less developed nations. Heralding *Article 25* intrinsically calls for redistribution of a breadth and scale unlike anything we have seen or known before. Through the collective pooling of a nation's wealth and resources and its redistribution according to human need, on a global as well as a national basis, it is possible that many other critical problems will be solved in a much shortened period of time.

For example, if *Article 25* had been implemented in all world regions many decades ago, then perhaps certain extremist and terrorist groups, like Al-Qaeda and ISIL, would never have come into existence. If every family in poor countries had already been given the material basis for trust and security in society, perhaps there would be no receptivity among the youth for violent religious ideologies, and no reason for them to fight against the government and overthrow its (no longer wholly corrupted) administration. And if an emergency programme had already been instituted to end hunger and extreme deprivation through massive resource transfers, extensive agrarian reforms and a major restructuring of the global economic architecture, then perhaps governments would have realised in practise the unalloyed benefits of international cooperation. And thus perhaps they would have long ago embarked on resolving the other looming threats to humanity's future that only genuine cooperation can accomplish, leading to an eventual abandonment of the drive for war and concerted, unsurpassed efforts to limit carbon emissions and heal the environment.

Indeed if we had shared the world's resources and eradicated global poverty, *especially* hunger, perhaps the environmental problems of today would have been kept to a minimum, and global development patterns would have taken a very different and more sustainable course. In many ways, the sorry fate of the environment was sealed after the Cancun Summit in 1981 when the gathered political leaders failed to agree upon Brandt's proposals, which historians of the future may discern to be the turning point for all that has followed. If only Mother Earth could talk, she may have said to those assembled heads of state: 'So you refuse to cooperate, and you don't want to share my plentiful riches that I give to you freely and in trust? Then don't blame me for the consequences of your own actions!'

Reagan and Thatcher and their coterie may well have scoffed at the summit's proceedings, but now they have gone we are all paying testament to the results of their decision to ignore Brandt's call to action, choosing instead to unleash the forces of commercialisation and follow their divisive path of separation, greed and selfish competition. In the intervening years successive governments have increasingly allowed market forces to become a rampant influence in social, economic and political affairs. They have together forsaken their responsibilities to govern on behalf of the common good, instead relinquishing their decision-making powers to the vagaries of the global marketplace. And they have effectively turned their backs on the United Nations and its founding vision, instead pursuing their power games through a Security Council that makes a mockery of international law. The inevitable result of these combined factors is a speeding up of environmental ruin, to the point we have reached today when two emergencies threaten the future prospects of our race—both extreme inequality and climate change—whereas at the time of the Cancun Summit we could have primarily concentrated on the former.

From the most self-interested perspective it would still have made sense to prioritise the elimination of poverty in order to prevent the escalation of environmental problems, presuming our political leaders held a long-term vision of a sustainable and peaceful world. Above all, it is well known that poverty is an underlying factor behind the rapid population growth of the past 60 or 70 years. If this trend persists throughout the coming century as predicted, there will obviously be serious repercussions for the environment, not least in terms of the increased consumption of resources in developing countries and consequently rising CO_2 emissions. While it is true that the people of rich nations consume the majority of global resources and therefore have the biggest impact on the environment, there is no denying the fact that a continued population explosion could lead to an untenable strain on the resource-base and ecological system of the earth. But there is enough evidence to show that population levels decrease and stabilise when families enjoy an adequate standard of living, which can only be truly understood through empathising with the psychology of the very poor. There are profoundly sad reasons why those who live in poverty often have many babies, mainly in the hope that some of their children—if they don't die early from malnutrition or preventable diseases—will help support their parents in old age. These ingrained cultural attitudes in developing countries can only be changed once every citizen has complete trust and faith that their government will guarantee, at all times, the fulfilment of their basic human needs as summarised in *Article 25*.

Witnessing the dramatic rise in global population levels that have taken place already during the twentieth century, one might imagine that governments would have wholeheartedly committed themselves to ameliorating the conditions that perpetuate this state of affairs, and given the utmost consideration to the fight against poverty, disease and undernourishment, along with all necessary international assistance and support of population programmes. We have now reached a time when the interrelated growth of poverty and the human population has become extremely perilous, not only due to the strain on the global environment, but also due to the time bomb that is contained within this equation in terms of potentially devastating social, economic and political conflicts. But far from committing themselves to a sane course of long-term remedial action, our governments have continued to pursue the visionless path of commercialisation—a path that perversely relishes the rapid growth of the world's population, no matter the risks to the future of humanity provided they continue to increase the bottom line of wealthy corporations.

Herein lies the mystery behind the population conundrum that may make us question the real reasons why the world is so overcrowded, as now experienced in the big cities of every developed nation as well as within the developing world. Can we still say that poverty is the basic underlying cause, or is it the forces of commercialisation that are driving these trends in recent decades through the proliferation of social insecurity, inequality and uncontrollable migration—all in the name of creating more corporate profits and economic growth?

This line of reasoning may help us to perceive how the human population could have been kept to a sustainable rate if we had shared the world's resources since the creation of the United Nations, with far-reaching significances for the state of the environment. On one hand, there would no longer be the nightmarish vision of 11 billion people or more living on an overstretched and degraded planet by the end of the twenty-first century, which is a projection that is by no means inevitable and could still be averted by first of all implementing *Article 25* across the world, especially in the very poorest regions as an urgent international priority. On the other hand, we have also discussed how implementing *Article 25* would pose a direct challenge to the forces of commercialisation for all of the reasons outlined previously, meaning that the drive for profit would no longer continue to be such a destructive factor within society or the environment, for indeed the profit motive apparently abhors the earth and humanity itself. Through the worldwide process of resource sharing, wealth redistribution and international cooperation towards the imperative goal of implementing *Article 25*, there is every reason to believe that multinational corporations would soon have to function in a more humane, socially benevolent and environmentally conscious manner.

Who can deny that this is for the benefit of all of us, including the corporate executives who are compelled, as part of their fiduciary duty to shareholders, to inadvertently destroy the environment by direct or indirect means? Is it possible that unless we do manage to implement *Article 25* very speedily, maybe there is no other way to prevent these large corporate entities from accelerating their rabidly destructive activities? For the only way for them to continue making their excessive profit margins is by further ravaging the natural world, even against their better judgement as they too begin to see the dreadful impacts within the planet's biosphere. So long as these purblind commercial forces are the reigning influence in global affairs, there is no doubt that the environment will deteriorate to the point that it is unfit for human habitation, while even modest proposals for sharing the world's wealth—like universal social protection—will become increasingly idealistic, unattainable and ultimately utopian.

Yet many people of goodwill still fail to recognise that there can be no solution to the environmental emergency in today's world without also dealing with the emergency of endemic hunger and poverty. Let us therefore try to recognise why it doesn't make any sense to fight for the rights of Mother Earth, if in the meantime we overlook the basic rights of a vast number of impoverished humanity. The simple logic can be surmised from what we have already reasoned above, for there are two kinds of environment, both natural and human, and each one is interdependent with the other. The forests, land, oceans, atmosphere and so on are what we normally understand as the sum total of the natural environment, but we should also consider the health of the sum total of the *human* environment as a causal factor for all that is going wrong in this world.

According to this understanding, the millions of people who are subsisting in severe poverty are the worst possible human environmental disaster, one that has determined the outcome of our wider ecological problems after being ashamedly tolerated for so many years. Therefore the environmentalist has made a critical error of judgement, because if we could turn back the clock to 1950 and restore the health of our human environment by first of all implementing *Article 25*, then the health of our planet would be far less precarious in the present day. Wealth and resources would have been more equitably distributed to meet the basic needs of all; purely profit-driven interests would have been necessarily relegated to their appropriate place; population levels in countries of the Global South may have eventually stabilised and started to decrease; and a restructured international economy may have led to more simple, sustainable and egalitarian lifestyles in the highly industrialised nations.

We are not blaming environmentalists for the world's problems or denigrating their vital work, but together we are trying to understand why most people do not readily perceive the causal link between poverty and environmental issues. Could it be that if poverty exists on this planet on an enormous scale, then environmental problems will surely follow in an almost mysterious way? And is it possible that the prevalent reality of poor families is reflected in the reality of poor climatic conditions? For what has led to this poverty in a world of plenty if not the drive for profit and power based on human greed, indifference and ignorance—

the same factors that have led multinational corporations to pillage the earth in the name of economic growth and consumerism. If we look carefully there is an inseparable connection between the environmental and poverty crises, which might be illustrated in diagrammatic form as a triangle with the words 'climate change', 'hunger/poverty' and 'population growth' in the respective corners, and 'profit/commercialisation' in the middle. In the process of making more profits through unbridled commercialisation, more poverty is created alongside more havoc within the atmosphere. And the more that poverty levels increase, the more the population of the world increases in tandem—leading the forces of commercialisation to grow in power and intensify these self-destructive trends forevermore.

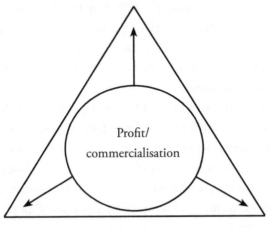

Climate Change

Profit/
commercialisation

Population
Growth

Hunger/
Poverty

Hence so long as the people of the world are not demanding the universal implementation of *Article 25* through the sharing of global resources, then so long will the drive for commercial profit continue to destroy our natural environment. And while the produce of the world is not shared, while food surpluses are left to rot while millions of people go hungry, while the human family continues to overlook the suffering of its poorest members, then it is inevitable that disequilibrium will be experienced in the planet's eco-systems and weather patterns. Because you cannot deal with environmental problems without also dealing with the injustice of poverty, the injustice of human exploitation, the injustice of hoarding and not sharing the earth's produce that belongs to us all. Is it therefore sufficient to bring awareness to the public about the climate crisis, without even mentioning the word 'hunger' or the lack of sharing in our world? Or is that the definition of our ignorance, considering that the planet's health is getting worse and worse the more we try to tackle environmental problems while paying insufficient attention to widespread human deprivation?

On solely moral grounds it is deplorable to believe we can tackle our environmental problems without also tackling global poverty, for there is no reason why we cannot save the hungry at the same time as we act to save our world. We now see many popular mobilisations to stop climate change or halt environmental destruction, but how often do we see coordinated worldwide actions that call for an *immediate end* to life-threatening conditions of hunger and poverty? Yet if we can organise ourselves globally to try and stop an illegal war, or else to raise awareness of an impending ecological catastrophe that most world leaders are seeming to ignore, then we can surely organise massive international protests that are united in the cause of implementing *Article 25*— and motivated by an attitude of 'what about the others?'

Maybe we should sit back and ask ourselves why the climate issue has become so important in our households, whilst around 17 million people dying from poverty-related causes each year is of no real concern to our everyday lives. Is it more important for us to breathe clean air tomorrow than it is for the desperately poor person to eat a piece of bread today, notwithstanding that hunger was a daily reality for millions of people even before Greenpeace was born? We have maybe 10 or 15 years left to prevent catastrophic climate change, but how many years or even days remain for the destitute child who is slowly dying from malnutrition? These questions are raised in a spirit of protest from the present writer, who has never understood the answers and never will. The indignity of poverty has existed for much longer than our present-day problem of environmental pollution, but for some strange reason only the weather has found a voice in worldwide public demonstrations. As if the environment has been given a first class seat in global activism, whilst the poor do not even have a class to sit in. And the very poorest citizens themselves only rarely speak up about their plight, so conditioned are they—as always— to accept their fate or quietly die in abject poverty.

This altogether leaves us with a disturbing realisation if we suppose that wealthy nations could succeed in restoring their local environment to a balanced state, despite the continuation of disastrous weather patterns in Africa, Asia or other regions with a high incidence of poverty. For would we then think about the others and impel our governments to help them, or would we continue with our insular, indifferent and complacent way of life that is currently the norm? The fact is that environmental issues are mainly about ourselves, our future and our own children's lives, with far less consideration given for the kind of future that extremely poor children have in distant countries. We are educating our own children to think about the good of the environment, to recycle plastic and tins in a green box, but we have failed to teach them to think about the millions of other children who live in severe poverty overseas without even the privilege of eating a nutritious meal each day. When for every bottle that a child in an affluent nation recycles at home, possibly two children are at that moment dying from poverty-related causes somewhere else in the world.

Of course, raising awareness about environmental issues is unquestionably crucial and laudable, for the planet is in a state of disrepair and an adequate response from humanity has hardly begun. But perhaps we should again pause for a moment to ask ourselves: do I care more about climate change than the reality of global hunger, simply because I am influenced by other followers of a fashionable cause? Indeed how many times did I recycle my household waste products in the past week, and how many times did I spare a thought for the literally hundreds of thousands of people who needlessly died as a result of poverty over the same time period? If you had spoken to any one of those fatally impoverished people about the state of the environment before they passed away, you can be sure they would have said in response: 'I cannot think about the forests or CO2 emissions, I just want some food, clean water, healthcare, a sustainable livelihood and adequate housing!'

Again, let us not be mistaken for it is certainly the right thing to educate others about the environmental emergency, but we also have to ask ourselves what kind of education this is in a divided, anguished and morally reprehensible world. What kind of better life can we expect when commercialisation is taking over the agenda of every mainstream political party, when the unjust global economy is causing hardship and despair for countless families, when international tensions are leading to an epidemic of anxiety and depression, and when thousands of people are dying from poverty each day beneath the radar of public attention? Why do we want the environment to return to health at all, if the world continues along this same iniquitous course? We don't even have reliable statistics for how many people are hungry or silently suffering in absolute poverty, although we have access to an endless stream of data about changing weather patterns and flows of greenhouse gases that may affect the affluent nations. Perhaps this is no surprise when any public discussions about the environment are considered to be principled and civilised, whereas barely a word is spoken in polite conversation about the tragedy of those who continue to die from poverty in the world's darkest corners.

Yet even now, in the midst of so much weather chaos and financial turmoil, it is still possible for nations to combine their efforts in feeding the hungry, healing the sick, caring for the dispossessed and *at the same time* preventing runaway climate change and repairing the environment. Doing so has always been possible, for as long as the problems have ever existed. The only way that governments can achieve this unparalleled objective today, however, is through the right politicians getting elected into office with the world's people united behind them—and *that* is where the root of the problem lies as a result of our deeply ingrained apathy and complacency.

When observing world problems from the most holistic and spiritual perspective, it may be said that the climate crisis is the result of human intelligence going in the wrong way due to our collective worshipping of profit, wealth and power, which has consequently led to a generalised indifference towards the environmental commons. But everyone plays a part in this adverse reality, which compels us all to acknowledge how we have become caught in the trap of environment breakdown due to our mutual complicity in the causes of this defining issue of our time. The trap is that we believe 'there is little time left to save the planet', while all along we contribute to the processes that are escalating the self-destruction of the natural world. Due to our inadequate modes of education and our consequent lack of self-knowledge, we do not know ourselves or the purpose of our lives, hence we are easily influenced by the desire to become 'happy' in a blinkered and egocentric manner through our identification with materiality. And the forces of commercialisation are superbly adept at exploiting our ignorance and conformity in order to make money in every direction, as exemplified in the grossest terms by the frenzy of overconsumption at Christmas or the mindless shopping on Black Friday sales. Through our psychological need for security and happiness we are all susceptible to the conditioning of our society that compels us to become a 'somebody' who is better than others, or otherwise indoctrinates us to aspire to live in luxury with large houses, profligate consumption habits and extravagant holidays.

Can we follow how this translates into a global picture that is characterised by millions of business contracts and profit-seeking activities around the world, in conjunction with foreign policies based on aggressive competition for limited global resources, which overall has an ongoing and devastating impact on the environment? Individuals are educated to aspire to become a successful somebody, leading to self-interested attitudes and a certain indifference to others that is expressed on both national and international levels. And that accumulated self-interest is the pride and joy of multinational corporations, leading to mass patterns of over-consumption and the degradation of the natural environment.

In the final analysis, it is neither governments nor corporations that are the driving factor behind the cutting of rainforests, the strip mining for valuable minerals, the non-stop digging for fossil fuels and so on. More exactly, it is the people within each nation that have been educated to desire the high-consumption lifestyle that brings about this necessitated destruction, regardless of its effects on the people of other nations where the destruction occurs. As we have noted elsewhere, the materialistic and self-seeking idea of the American Dream has now been exported to almost every country of the world, and it represents a form of social conditioning that is not only synonymous with commercialisation but also with environmental ruination.[13] Observing this complex mess in its totality that we are all responsible for perpetuating to a greater or lesser degree, the question of man's culpability in causing global warming is a diversion to which we might as well reply: what does it matter anyway?

Reflecting on how we participate in prolonging today's climate crisis may also lead us to realise that a deeper cause of the problem originates in how we live together and interact within society. For we are born into a world where people are lacking in joy, are heavily conditioned and uncreative, are psychologically separated from one another in their relationships—all of which causes serious disequilibrium within the environment and atmosphere. Hence the prevalent motivation to become rich and successful in the midst of poverty and misery is also a cause of the disturbances that are felt within the elements of nature. This is an esoteric but essential insight to perceive if we want to understand why we can never heal the planet's ecosystems unless we also resolve our social problems in all their dimensions. In other words, it is not just what man *does* that affects the environment, but also what he *thinks* and *feels*, as there is an intricate relationship between man's thought and the natural world.

If you go into the room of a depressive or drug addict and it negatively affects you on a subtle or emotional level, then it is surely possible that all the negative thoughts and emotions of people in their masses has a deleterious effect on nature and global climatic conditions. And what is the predominant tenor of the thoughts that man is producing right now? What else but the idolatry of profit, power and wealth, mixed with an endemic indifference to the welfare of others. Greed *per se* represents imbalance, and if we extrapolate all the avarice, selfishness and indifference that is expressed within individuals to an aggregate level, then we can surmise the effect it may have on the life around us, including weather patterns, sea levels, and the behaviour of plants and animals.

So it is not only the worldly activities of multinational corporations that causes ecological destruction, but also the very *thought* and *intention* of corporate lobbying or pernicious deal-making by many millions of business executives. Similarly, a powerful government that sells armaments to other nations is not only responsible for perpetuating war and death in far-off regions, but also for spreading fear and depression in the consciousness of people throughout the world, which is ultimately reflected in disturbances within the planet's atmosphere and ecosystems. Even the apartheid walls around the West Bank and Gaza have a tremendously negative effect on the elements of nature, and ramify the psychological depression, anguish and hatred that is raging in our divided world. If there is a divine evolutionary plan for humanity, then such a wall represents its polar opposite and should be regarded as one of the ugliest monuments built in the late twentieth-century. For man is Life and every atom within the universe is inextricably connected, which is a basic postulate that has profound implications for societal arrangements and human relationships once we thoroughly apprehend and accept its validity.

Until then, we are all someway to blame for the continuation of both our social and environmental crises, and we are only truly united in terms of our ignorance or indifference to the links between these associated problems. Just as the transnational corporate entity is indifferent to the destruction it perpetrates on nature, we too are collectively indifferent to the millions of people who are at risk of dying as a result of hunger and other poverty-related causes. If the big corporation effectively abhors nature for the sake of profit, we effectively abhor our poorest brothers and sisters for the sake of pursuing our private happiness and comfort. Hence we are all the same in terms of our self-centredness, blindness, arrogance, ignorance and indifference. Yet for so long have we ignored the problem of man-made hunger and poverty, that now poverty is coming back to haunt us through social turmoil and disasters in the environment— because everything that happens on this earth is spiritually interrelated.

Have you noticed how the climate has suddenly deteriorated over the past few decades since commercialisation entered our veins, and humanity started consuming resources more fiercely than ever before? Have you noticed how rapidly the streets are becoming more crowded, how homelessness and poverty is getting worse by the day, how we are becoming more and more confused and exhausted from all the suffering, pain, and moral depravity of our world? And have you observed how this dysfunctional system that we mutually sustain has now developed a clever mechanism that reproduces itself, forcing us to remain caught in its divisive processes even if we don't want to be part of it anymore? Then know the truth that climate change is a reflection of the disorder that can be openly witnessed in our dysfunctional society today, born out of all the sorrow, injustice, greed, inequality, and most of all the *indifference* that is endemic on this planet. Reverse all of that and you will have a healthy environment, for as long as you shall live and beyond. For to be indifferent to hunger and poverty is to deny yourself those God-given moments of freedom where you gaze up at a deep blue sky in complete inner silence, where the climate is still dignified with its four seasons, and where the sea in its love never says no to the rivers of the world who want to enter its womb.

***

In perceiving that the primary causes of the environmental crisis are rooted in our consciousness and our relationships with each other, we may simply conclude that all of humanity's problems are the result of a lack of vision and love. It is not only the governments that are failing to listen to their own people, but it is we who are failing to listen to the voice of our own hearts. And this is the most severe pollution that threatens the future of the world, more so than carbon dioxide emissions in the atmosphere, for it is a pollution to the attributes of our hearts that also blinds us to common sense and reason. We know that rich elites have always seen the poor as a kind of social pollution that should be dealt with by eradicating the poor themselves, instead of eradicating the conditions that determine their deprivation. But we too ignore the attributes of our hearts as long as we continue to accept a state of affairs in which millions of people die in poverty, altogether needlessly and due to man-made causes in a world of plenty.

Do we have any empathy at all with the psychology of someone who lives for many years in abject poverty? To be so poor that you produce many children without the means to adequately provide for them, knowing that many are likely to die before they have a chance to live, means that you have already been let down by your community, forgotten by your society, and effectively abandoned by humanity itself. There is an acute sense of loss in the mind of such a man or woman, and a dreadful feeling of loneliness that only the desperately poor can experience—a sense of being totally unwanted, inwardly worthless and betrayed by God. That is the malefic effect of man's indifference to the suffering of the least fortunate among us, for when you are hopelessly disadvantaged, when you are living in misery and utter destitution, it makes you feel as if you are a human being without a soul. You cannot see any purpose in life. You neither like nor hate yourself. And the only emotion that you can experience is that of your heart crying out loud for help that never comes.

Such is the psychological reality that endures for millions of people each day in the poorest villages and city slums of many underdeveloped regions across the world. We may ourselves be kind and charitable, we may be filled with benevolence and virtuous intentions, but if we have never experienced that kind of poverty then we have no idea what it feels like to have no food for the next two weeks, without hope of government welfare or public support. The effect of our collective complacency and indifference is far graver than we might imagine, and we have yet to grasp its real implications within our cultural attitudes and conventional mores. To turn our backs on those people who are needlessly starving and destitute is effectively to deny the inviolability of their soul's divine purpose, and to deprive them of their God-given right to spiritually evolve—which is the greatest crime among all others that we are all guilty of committing, as this writer has repeatedly asserted before.

Please meditate upon what has just been said and then reflect again upon the content of *Article 25* in order to intuit for yourself what should now be done in your discussions, protests, communications and so forth. Every person from whatever background can play a role in this vast civilisational endeavour to urgently right the age-old wrong of hunger and poverty, whether it's through economic, political, social, artistic or even scientific means. What should be most prioritised in our thoughts and activism is not only ecological issues as they may affect us at home, but also our awareness of the interconnection between the global environmental and poverty crises which will lead us to realise that *sharing the world's resources* is the solution to humanity's problems on every level.

To go out on the streets and demonstrate for governments to tackle climate change is very different from demanding that the world's poor are fed and protected, since the latter represents the beginning of a transformation in our conscious awareness that is based on our compassion for those less fortunate than ourselves. It is to think 'what about the others?' through heartfelt empathetic concern, and to temporarily forget about one's own life and self-interested worries. It is to sense the holistic relatedness of all world problems, from which understanding we should ideally participate in every demonstration for social or climate justice that happens at any time. Ultimately, it is to know that humanity is One and justice *per se* cannot be divided, thus recognising that hunger is injustice itself because it affects the world as a whole, even in terms of weather chaos and a critically suffering planet.

Understanding the interconnectedness of world problems also means that we recognise our responsibility to talk and act as an ambassador for humanity, assuming that we are already equipped with goodwill, common sense and a growing awareness of right human relationship. Only our hearts can truly explain the importance of these insufficient terms, for our misapplied human intelligence has obfuscated the simple meaning of such words for millennia. It is not enough to educate our children in the importance of recycling household materials to protect the environment, for example, if we do not also educate them in the importance of recycling human life through global economic sharing and international cooperation. Otherwise we are limiting their conscious awareness to that recycling container, which has little to do with saving our planet unless we also teach them how our environmental problems first came about, as if that container was a Pandora's Box that links to every other global issue. This also means that parents have to educate themselves in what commercialisation is doing to the environment and what their government is doing to the world, so that they can lead by example in guiding their children to become an ambassador for humanity like themselves.

Therefore at the centre of our school education programmes of today should be an understanding of the need to secure every person's basic needs in every country, which doesn't only refer to the universal rights to food, healthcare, shelter and social security. Let's not restrict our understanding to the few sentences that define *Article 25* and instead use our intuition to read between the lines, for heralding *Article 25* in endless protests also implies a new awareness of our moral responsibility and vision for One World. What is happening through global demonstrations on the environment is in fact symbolic of the emerging recognition that humanity is One, and it represents the beginning of world consciousness and the coming rejection of our long divided past. In this respect, climate change is a great teacher who is trying to unite the people of the world for a shared planetary cause, so that we may finally come to realise the significance of our spiritual oneness and interrelatedness. But the fact that there are no worldwide public demonstrations to end hunger and life-threatening poverty also means that we are still moving in the wrong direction, and we have yet to realise *en masse* how sharing the world's resources is the *only* pathway for reversing environmental destruction, for commencing a simpler way of life, and for establishing a sustainable economy based on the common good of all.

PART IV

Engaging the heart

We have now explored some key reasons why implementing *Article 25* is of the utmost importance to the crucial years ahead, and why the responsibility for world transformation rests with a united voice of ordinary engaged citizens. Considering how grave is the extent of the inequality, environmental and security crises that face us today, it would be naïve or foolish to believe that our governments will suddenly awaken to reality and begin to steer the world onto a more stable course. Billions of dollars continue to be poured into senseless wars and destructive geopolitical stratagems in spite of unpayable national debts and escalating wealth inequalities, while the policies of most heads of state are further commercialising all that remains of the public's commonly shared assets.

Even following a global financial crisis that required public bail-outs of private banking institutions which had brought the world economy to its knees, still the lesson of international solidarity has not been learnt towards the mutual objective of social and planetary renewal. Each nation has again turned its back on the rest and shown a lack of real concern for the earth's suffering, instead of finally helping one another and working together in a spirit of genuine cooperation and economic sharing. We may draw an analogy from what the Israeli government is doing to the Palestinian people, and compare the oppression of their neighbours with the subjugation that is inflicted on the world as a whole by powerful countries through their brutal foreign policies, along with multinational corporations and their profit-driven tyranny. What will wake them all up to the suffering they are inflicting on vulnerable peoples and less developed nations, and when will they learn the simple lesson to treat their poorer brethren with decency, kindness and affection?

Alas we are deluded if we believe that vested interests will suddenly stop their lobbying and cease thieving the world's resources for their own benefit, just as we are credulous if we believe that the Israeli government will end its aggression that continues under the cover of that duplicitous phrase, 'the peace process'. There are only two hopes for ending this enduring and worsening impasse in world affairs; either a wishful and passive plea for divine intervention, or a concerted awakening of ordinary people who stand together in their millions to say: NO MORE AND NEVER AGAIN!

Notwithstanding the former possibility, there are certain preconditions to be met if a united people's voice is ever to grow in sufficient strength and stature that it is capable of influencing government decisions and reorienting the currently disastrous world direction. First of all, it is necessary to repeat that there must be a constant presence of millions of people in the streets worldwide who resoundingly espouse the human rights of *Article 25*, and whose presence must continue unceasingly throughout the day and night *ad infinitum*. Indeed if something is seriously wrong with your physical body, you don't go into hospital for just one day, but for a very long period of time until the process of healing has completed its natural course. Correspondingly, the body of humanity is in such a critical condition that the only cure is for countless people of goodwill to gather in the streets, and to peacefully protest for a turnaround in governmental priorities as if the future of the world depends on it—which in a literal sense it does. When the time has come and ordinary citizens embrace the same cause in every country and across different continents, then perhaps we can seriously envision millions of people in each capital city congregated in unison, day after day and week after week in ever renewing numbers.

We must admire in this respect the various Occupy protesters who may still be camping in central squares if the police had not forcefully evicted them, which was only possible because those stalwart activists comprised but a small percentage of the national population. Thus it was relatively easy for the authorities to stamp out their hopes and aspirations, rendering them into a lonely group of frustrated people who valiantly tried to do the job of all their fellow citizens. But what will the government do if a significant majority of the nation joins these unremitting protests that are hereon predicated on implementing *Article 25*, repeatedly amassing and replenishing themselves in such multitudes that the police will be incapable of repressing or containing them?

There's no question that establishment politicians, police departments and wealthy elites are carefully watching the new protest movements each time they manifest, and they continue to reassure themselves by thinking: 'They'll surely calm down and go home eventually like they did last time, and then it will be back to business-as-usual'. So we have to reach the stage when ordinary people from every walk of life join in with this resurgence of nonviolent protest, including families who have never protested before as well as schoolchildren and public sector workers, at which point even the police may turn towards the government and say: 'I'm not with you, I'm with the people!'

We should be clear by now on what we need to demand from our respective governments, which is much more than raising the minimum wage at home or giving increased aid to developing countries. The continued fight for a paltry 'minimum' wage reflects a long and dark history of human exploitation, corporate theft and public indifference, and it has no real relationship to *Article 25* which must eventually be translated into a far more comprehensive set of laws that guarantee everyone's right to a fair and decent standard of living. How can we move in our societies today amidst all the wealth that is unequally distributed, and yet only demand the barest minimal standard of living for the struggling poor majority?

If we are able to read between the lines as suggested, then *Article 25* really means the end of the old ways based on selfishness, greed and theft, and the beginning of common sense and a new way of life based on goodwill, sharing, justice and thence right human relations. It means that no elected leader can remain in office without following the public's determination to end all forms of poverty both nationally and globally, not on the basis of an ideology but on terms of basic dignity and morality. As we have briefly reasoned heretofore, once the human rights of *Article 25* are firmly guaranteed by all governments it will represent an antidote to the increasing stranglehold of commercialisation, to the wanton plundering and destruction of multinational corporations, and to the insanity of foreign policies that are predicated on aggression and power politics. If only we could personify those materialistic forces of commercialisation, then we might picture them scratching their heads in the midst of millions of people calling for *Article 25* throughout the world, before they quietly whisper to each other: 'We're really in trouble this time'.

Thus to herald *Article 25* as the leading people's cause is the path of least resistance, and it may quickly lead to many positive results and a new social settlement that we cannot currently anticipate. Within its simple requirements for every human being are embedded all the demands of progressive activists down the ages, even in terms of environmental justice as we have now discussed in the foregoing chapter. There's no longer the time to compile a long list of radical demands that governments should accede to, which is not an inclusive way to transform the world when such demands will lead to revolution after revolution if forcefully pursued in the volatile context of our polarised societies. Many young activists today are complicating matters with their manifestos for political and economic transformation, almost as if they are imitating what we call 'the system' and trying to engage with its labyrinthine processes, instead of diminishing its power by gathering with millions of other people in permanent protests across the world. Let's not forget that the system is extremely old and malefic in its divisive complexity, as it has always been since before we were born, hence to try and negotiate with the system's representatives on their own terms is futile and never-ending. Just as the well-intentioned politician who tries to reform government from within is liable to be reformed from within himself, so may the lonely activist who tries to change the system eventually find that the system has changed them.

So let's take the path of least resistance and jointly herald *Article 25*, knowing that this is the surest route for impelling our governments to redistribute resources and restructure the global economy. Such a demand can be expressed in our own creative ways, safe in the knowledge that it holds within itself all the answers we are trying to find. Then we may realise that many existing demands of global activists are already embodied within the *Universal Declaration of Human Rights*, including in wealthy countries where the call for sharing is now being expressed in an incipient form. Observe in this regard the diverse movements for accessible social housing, for the public control of utilities and transportation, for the free provision of healthcare and higher education, or for a more equal and redistributive society through fair taxation. There is no doubt that the principle of sharing must be institutionalised within each nation along these preliminary lines, and it is natural that engaged citizens are engrossed with the furtherance of these issues in their own societies. But we also have to be aware that our problems are essentially the same as those of other nations, for it is that awareness which will bring us together and make us into an implacable (although *peaceful*) international force.

This new global awareness is in fact the essence of a people's strategy in heralding *Article 25*, because it should not be demonstrated for in one country alone but always in many different countries at the same time. As earlier discussed in relation to the issue of economic growth and social prosperity, we have finally reached a point when *planetary group work* is necessary to resolve humanity's problems, which are manifestly international in scope and can no longer be tackled on a strictly national or unilateral basis. That is why the responsibility that rests with engaged citizens is to firstly read between the lines as to the meaning of *Article 25*, and then out of that awareness to mobilise across one's own country with the express intention of calling upon other nations to follow suit.

Remaining cognisant of the fact that our overall objective is for *Article 25* to be instituted as a presiding law within each country, it means that we want to empower the United Nations to ensure that all governments of the world uphold these laws, in whatever way such statutes are enshrined. We have noted how the present situation is clearly the reverse in most countries, where governments continue to pursue those harmful policies that unravel social protection guarantees and compromise the fulfilment of many people's essential needs. But if *Article 25* was established as an abiding and foundational law for every country, then perhaps the police would have to arrest the politicians instead of curtailing the peaceful protests of ordinary people, most of whom are fighting to defend their basic human rights that should always have been protected by the United Nations.

From this understanding we may realise that the correct strategy for world transformation is not to call upon our national governments alone, who as we know are often failing to safeguard the common welfare of all their citizens. At the same time we must call upon the United Nations to truly represent the people of the world, which is a call that must be voiced on an intercontinental scale if it is to be lastingly effective. After all, when a government is oppressed by another country it has the opportunity to bring its case before the International Court of Justice, but where does such representation exist for the world's poorest families and individuals? Unsurprisingly, there is nowhere they can go to seek recourse for the injustice of their poverty, even when governments are bailing out wealthy banking institutions following an international collapse of the global economy.

So we need a United Nations that represents the hearts and minds of the world's people, and that gives the highest priority of all to the needs of the unheard and dying poor. Even if we ourselves have guaranteed access to our essential needs, who are we going to complain to when our governments are attacking the public institutions and social services that we hold most dear, with scant regard for our long-established human rights and basic entitlements for life and liberty? We may passionately disagree with the free trade agreements and privatisations that are further commercialising every aspect of our lives, for example, but how are we going to create a better world when our governments are working on behalf of corporations instead of prioritising our most fundamental social concerns?

This is another reason why we need to work with an article that belongs to the *Universal Declaration of Human Rights*, because these commonly-agreed standards of achievement for all nations are never going to be realised unless the world's people continually advocate for them through huge popular mobilisations, out of which process a country leader may finally begin to listen to their constituents and act faithfully in accordance. Although that is very unlikely to be one of the leaders of most existing government administrations, so we should regard the United Nations as the true president of all humanity and our paramount hope for bailing out the world's poor. When there is conflict within a particular world region and no immediate solutions are to be found, then the United Nation's blue helmets go in as a peacekeeping force to monitor events and seek a resolution, however impotent their presence may be in supposedly representing the manifest will of the community of nations. Now imagine that the United Nations begins to represent the manifest will of all the world's citizens, and is thereby empowered through a global outpouring of public support to act upon the people's mandate for implementing *Article 25*. Assuredly it won't be long before the United Nations sends its emissaries to Washington, Brussels, Moscow and every other government headquarters to say: 'We have waited long enough—it's time to feed and protect the world's starving and impoverished people!'

The youth may soon realise that heeding this course of action will make an amazing amount of noise around the world, leading to extraordinary results that take place within a social atmosphere that we have never seen or experienced before. What we want most of all is to give a new lease of life to the United Nations, and if millions of people are protesting non-stop every day and night, month after month and even year after year for the formidable cause of implementing *Article 25*, then we may eventually witness a considerable empowerment of the United Nations General Assembly and a gradual weakening of the Security Council. As reasoned previously, a reformed and fully democratic United Nations system has a major role to play in overseeing the management of a restructured global economy. However, its intended function in this regard—as spelled out in Article 55 of its Charter—cannot be fulfilled until it is freed from the constraints of the Security Council veto, freed from the influence of the corporate-dominated Bretton Woods institutions, and freed from its funding limitations through far greater and more reliable sources of revenue. The United Nations does not belong to political or corporate interests in America, China, France, Russia or the United Kingdom—it belongs to us all, which is the envisioned purpose of its existence in promoting 'the economic and social advancement of all peoples'.

With this in mind, the youth of America should ask themselves why they were protesting outside Wall Street and proclaiming the rights of 'the 99%', instead of gathering around the United Nations Headquarters and heralding *Article 25*. Declaring 'We are the 99%' leads to nowhere at the end of the day, but if we call for *Article 25* then the poor will eventually hear us and join in—and *that* is where the solution lies! Imagine if you speak about Occupy Wall Street to the very poorest people in regions such as sub-Saharan Africa, rural China or India, then how do you think they will respond to your nationwide concerns? Explain to them how the global economy functions, and they will probably not know what you mean. Explain to them the meaning of credit default swaps or quantitative easing, and they probably won't understand a word. There are many people in the poorest slums and villages who have never even heard of the word 'capitalism'. But if you read to them the contents of *Article 25* then you can be sure their eyes would light up and they would understand right away, because then you are talking about *their* lives as well as your own.

These issues of inequality and injustice have always belonged to the poor, before they were appropriated and overcomplicated by intellectuals. The complex problems of the world are the problems of the poor too, so are we going to talk on their behalf or are we going to invite them to speak for themselves? The very poorest citizens are used to living with their mouths shut however difficult and undeserved their circumstances, even to the point where they quietly die in squalor and misery as we have noted before. But when they hear the call for change as expressed through millions of people decrying the senselessness of their poverty, then they will see the alternative in their minds as if they knew it already, for *Article 25* should have been implemented a long time ago as far as they are concerned.

To understand this for ourselves we have to look at the reality of poverty inwardly and psychologically, not intellectually or through the eyes of complacency, which means we must 'be with' the poor both spiritually and emotionally in order to see how *Article 25* is an alternative within itself. When millions of ordinary people of goodwill demand an end to poverty in continuous global demonstrations, then that alternative will come alive and speak for the very first time. Subsequent political and economic reforms will ensue at such a fast pace that many negative global trends will start to reverse, including that of the rich getting ever richer due to their increasing concentration of wealth and power, which will at least allow humanity some time to breathe, as it were, when nations begin to cooperate in redistributing essential resources to the poorest regions of the world.

Humanity has long been asking for *Article 25* to be implemented worldwide in different ways, such as through the activities of non-governmental organisations like the Red Cross or Oxfam. Yet these piecemeal and charitable efforts will never be sufficient unless the masses of the world stand firmly behind them, thus obliging governments to fully utilise their ample resources and decisively play their allotted role. So let the poor join in! Let other nations join in! Let common sense join in! Are we not tired of protesting in vain and participating in demonstrations where only a few thousand people are engaged with a just cause? Then let's together herald *Article 25* and see what happens, because if you're persistently standing in the streets for an end to hunger and life-threatening poverty then millions of other people will soon enough join you, no matter their nationality or where they live in the world. Maybe even the tourists in capital cities will throw away their guidebooks and stand beside you, especially if the time has finally come. Poverty is poverty wherever it exists in the world, and injustice is injustice whatever your social status or country of birth.

To hail 'the 99%' in rich nations alone is therefore the wrong language and the wrong strategy, for it may imply that injustice has been Westernised and doesn't belong to the rest of humanity. A majority of the very poorest people have still never heard of those Occupy protests that swept across many countries in 2011 and 2012, and even if they did sympathise with those various national causes it wasn't their place to get involved. But to protest for an end to poverty *per se* is a worldwide calling in which everyone has a role, so let's appeal to the poor by heralding *Article 25* and thereby build a colossal army. Let's not only talk about the need for social justice in our own country, but also communicate among ourselves internationally about the urgency of ensuring that everyone has their basic needs met *immediately*, which as we know can definitely be accomplished for there are more than enough resources to go around.

We can creatively illustrate this simple fact in our varied campaigning endeavours, for example by researching common-sense statistics that reveal how much food is in surplus or wasted within each country. Alternatively, we can demonstrate how easily governments and civil society can deliver the essentials of life to each person unconditionally, via new global economic arrangements that pool and redistribute surplus resources without being hindered by the profit imperative. Through innovative thinking and countless direct actions, let's call upon our governments to respect and listen to 'we the people of the United Nations', until a central proposal contained within the Brandt Report comes back to the negotiating table: for an emergency programme to abolish hunger and malnutrition through the elimination of absolute poverty as a global priority above all priorities.

Let's also be aware, however, that it's impossible to transform the world by continually fighting against 'capitalism' or 'the system', which is not only because many uneducated poor people are unlikely to understand such a complex and belligerent cause. The term 'capitalism' itself is misleading and divisive, and there is in fact no such entity called 'the system' that we can actively oppose—there are only people in the world who hide behind ideas or abuse principles for their own devious intentions. Capitalism is just an idea, a principle, which has been hijacked over several centuries by wealthy and political elites who manipulate laws and policies to serve their self-interest, often in the name of a 'democracy' or 'freedom' that they do not understand and which has nothing to do with them.

So let's not be fooled when others point at capitalism and blame the system for the world's problems, for the *principle* of capitalism *per se* is in no way synonymous with injustice, inequality or the super-rich. What we call the system does not exist apart from the human intentions that have created and sustained it, the mainstay of which are characterised by ambition, greed, selfishness and even cruelty. Hence the system in its totality is largely unfair, selfish, indifferent and often cruel. When we look at the financial turmoil and injustice in the world, it isn't capitalism we see but the consequences of certain individuals' motivations who are ignorant about the spiritual purpose of life and lacking in common sense, even lacking in love for themselves. We see too many people who are chasing money, power and prestige, and too few who are truly concerned about serving humanity and safeguarding the welfare of others.

This is not to imply that the present writer is defending capitalism; on the contrary, for we can say the same about the principles of socialism or communism. What's inherently wrong with capitalism as a principle? Nothing. What's inherently wrong with communism as a principle? Nothing, however corrupted and distorted was this essentially spiritual idea by authoritarian regimes or power-hungry leaders. Neither the principles of capitalism nor socialism have yet been demonstrated in anything near to their true form of social organisation, and they can never be so until the principle of sharing is implemented in world affairs on the basis of right human relations. Thus it is futile for the ordinary person to identify with these misunderstood terms and titles, as it is not principles that are to blame for world problems but only man himself. Only man can change, not capitalism or the system, for the system is merely a product of man's thoughts and actions. The system *per se* doesn't exist—only people exist. And yet, because the society we have created is so divided and unjust, we strangely blame 'the system' for our discontentment and unhappiness, which is an erroneous and potentially dangerous conclusion to reach.

We need to look at the principles underlying socialism and capitalism in a different light and with a more spiritual understanding, not according to the old ways of humanity that are based on partisan politics and never-ending conflict. A political movement that is 'against' the establishment and wants to replace it with another 'ism' will never succeed in advancing the common good of all, and will never include the very poorest people who are not interested in being a socialist, a communist, a libertarian or anything else; they only want to feed their family and enjoy a secure and peaceful way of life. By standing in opposition to capitalism or the corrupt system, we are therefore engaging in those old divisive processes that have led to class conflict and social marginalisation over and over again for hundreds of years.

It's almost as if activists are trying to personify capitalism in their minds and kill it with a knife, when in reality a theory or principle can never be killed. We can only understand the truth of what is happening, which is really a war brought about by the forces of commercialisation that has nothing do with 'capitalism' at all. So when you try and fight capitalism, you fight against an idea instead of effectively challenging or engaging with the elites that sustain the status quo. And in so doing, you are in danger of becoming just as divisive as they are. At best, the authorities will take one look at those protesters who call themselves 'anti-capitalists' and sweep them away without a second thought, for such activism has only ever comprised a small and often militant faction of the population. At worst, however, any popular movement that is 'against' the existing social order could eventually lead to riots, chaos and a violent uprising with even more terrible social and political outcomes.

To assert 'we need a revolution' in our polarised modern societies is therefore an inane and reckless suggestion, because the word revolution breeds the word enemy, which breeds the word against; and the internal attitude of being 'against' breeds mental blindness and selfishness in its turn. The psychological counterpart of thinking 'I'm against you' is stubbornness, arrogance and violence (whether expressed inwardly or outwardly), and it invariably hardens people's hearts and leads to fragmentation and conflict, both on an individual and societal level. The word revolution is outdated for the coming era in every respect, and now is the time for a new dispensation based on cooperation, goodwill, sharing and global unity—as well as copious amounts of common sense!

Heeding this we will hopefully perceive the futility of calling for an alternative to capitalism *as a principle* in our societies, and instead advocate for an alternative to our present modes of education that are an originating cause of world problems. From the start of life, all children need to be educated in terms of right human relationship, with a cultivated awareness that humanity is one interdependent family in which everyone's needs are basically the same wherever we live in the world or whatever language we speak, and however seemingly different our outer forms of social organisation. Right education also requires a common understanding that the principles of sharing and cooperation must underlie our economic structures and practices, as this basic knowledge represents the first step towards resolving entrenched social divisions and dissolving opposing modes of ideological thought.

A new era could begin immediately if enough people re-educate themselves and eliminate from their consciousness the pervasive conditioning of political 'isms', as often defined by the ill-considered terms 'left-wing' and 'right-wing'. The need for such an education is a vast subject that requires much reflection and further consideration, for we have imprisoned our minds over untold centuries through wrong conditioning and identification with 'isms' in all their diverse forms, leading to the most damaging repercussions for human creativity and freedom. It is the ordinary man and woman who has always suffered the most harmful consequences of this gross infringement of human free will throughout the centuries, as chiefly imposed by the major religious and political ideologies that still vie for dominance in world affairs.

We can only begin to understand the enormity of the problem by contemplating our prevalent psychological attitude of being 'against' capitalism or socialism or any other perceived ideological enemy. Nevertheless, this is a fruitful place to begin understanding the new awareness that must facilitate human relationships in the years to come. We should firstly relinquish any identification in our minds with the terms 'left-wing', 'right-wing', 'capitalism', 'socialism', 'anarchism', 'liberalism' and all the rest of it, while the word 'against' should be irrevocably replaced in our vocabulary and thinking with the words 'not with'. To think 'I'm against you' invariably leads to hostility or violence, but to think 'I'm not with you' infers the possibility of dialogue and resolution without undue conflict. More significantly, a mindset of inclusiveness and unity understands that there is no real psychological division between you or I, which may help us to recognise how we are spiritually connected as human beings even if we diverge in our social attitudes and mental ideations. Humanity is forever one in its essence and there can be no separation between us in the highest spiritual sense, however divided we may appear to be on the physical plane. Thus if there appears to be an irreconcilable conflict between opposing political ideologies, the lasting solution lies not in the victory of one 'ism' over another, but must be found in what can unite us all through a universal acceptance of our shared humanity—which ultimately requires a new education into the true nature of the inner Self.

There is nothing sentimental or naïve about these suggestions as such an attitude to human relationships has the potential to transform society once a bulk of the population is educated to think and become aware of themselves in a more spiritual, heart-engaged and inclusive way. It would soon be obvious that capitalism today is predominantly sustained by wealthy elites with an attitude of 'there is only the one me', instead of 'there is only the One Humanity'. To go very close psychologically to our present-day understanding of capitalism is actually to observe how its various forms of social organisation are characterised by greed and a lack of love, and little else. When man becomes aware of that and changes his intentions accordingly, then capitalism will change its outer expression in exactly the same measure. Through the institutionalised process of sharing resources both nationally and internationally, it is inevitable that capitalism will gradually assume a less dominant and purer form of expression. Until eventually, capitalism will be based on the sharing of innovation instead of the unchecked rule of market forces, within the context of a socially managed economy that prioritises the universal provision of essential goods and services.

Perhaps the only way to initiate these changes within our consciousness and across our societies is to herald *Article 25* in endless demonstrations and peaceful mass gatherings, which could eventually open the door to transforming both capitalism and socialism into their respectively appropriate forms for an age of sharing, justice and global cooperation. However, it is worth reflecting further for oneself on the fact that *Article 25* has nothing to do with the principles of either socialism or capitalism *per se*, for it is solely associated with the principle of *right human relationship* in the sense of enabling everyone on this earth to spiritually evolve with dignity and in freedom.

Whatever our ideological leanings or predilections, let's at least realise that rising up against capitalism is an absurdity that comes down to an idea fighting an idea, and let's instead be pragmatic by heralding one demand that can transcend our political differences in the most inclusive way. We need one unifying demand, not thousands of disparate and isolated causes. Moreover, fighting against capitalism alienates the non-politicised public and inhibits widespread popular participation, whereas heralding *Article 25* can unite humanity as a whole and invite everyone to realise their untapped potential as a leader. We may be amazed to find out what happens when millions of people unite without the energy of being 'against', because it will bring such inspiration and joy to onlookers that millions more people will soon join in. How simple indeed we may find the solution to world problems in the end, despite all the complexity of their manifestation and all the libraries of books that continue to be written about them.

The solution does not require intellectual output or complicated academic theories, but simply the hearts of ordinary people to be engaged in spontaneous, ceaseless, peaceful and unbelievably huge demonstrations that revolve around the human rights of *Article 25*. Dedicated activists should eschew altogether that menacing word 'revolution', and instead think in terms of creating an army of the heart which is the guaranteed route towards unifying people worldwide like never before. It's time to speak via the heart, not via the old ideologies and isms. We cannot transform the world through the word 'disobedience', the word 'against', or the word 'anti', but we can transform the world beyond our imagining by communicating from heart to heart for a new dispensation. When a substantial segment of every society joins in this collective endeavour and persistently calls for *Article 25*, the energy of those peaceful demonstrations will bring about the revelation of a new earth that humanity is now preparing for, albeit unconsciously in the main. Through the sound of those worldwide protest gatherings with the heart engaged, and with the commitment of millions of people who demonstrate continually every day, the question of 'how' to transform the world will naturally be revealed and nothing will stop those transformations from taking place.

We could accurately say that the greatest adversary of our rotten and corrupt system is the human heart, as the heart is so simple in its attributes and yet it becomes astonishingly powerful when it joins with other hearts in a common cause. In the same way as our heart is engaged to look after our children or protect our family, we need to infuse popular demonstrations with the same awareness and unwavering concern for the horrendous poverty that is experienced by millions of families and destitute individuals, many of whom are at risk of dying from hunger or preventable diseases at this very moment. Most activists and progressive thinkers have failed to recognise the power of massed goodwill as a prerequisite for global transformation, but without awakening the hearts of ordinary people there is no hope of engaging the public in any endeavour to make the world a better place, particularly at this critical stage of humanity's evolution that is compromised from all sides by the war of isms and commercialisation.

If we must talk of revolution then let it be a revolution of the heart, which is far from the old conditioning of isms that is still apparent in political discourse about the Arab Spring and its attendant uprisings. The strategy for world renewal that we are here considering is not the same as the public uprisings that happened in Egypt and other Middle Eastern countries from 2011, which were principally concerned with ending the reign of authoritarian and corrupt political regimes. Such a stand against repressive rulers is the cause of the people of that particular nation; I may sympathise but I am unlikely to get involved unless it's happening in my own country. But to stand for an end to poverty wherever it exists is the cause of every nation and the people of the whole world, and it will require a worldwide revolution of the heart if it is ever to succeed.

This proposition highlights a central dilemma that activists should contemplate and try to understand: to fight for change and justice is undeniably necessary and admirable, but to fight with a mind that is conditioned by isms and ideology is a dangerous undertaking that could lead to an even worse situation. In the mechanism of that conditioning lives the repetition of humanity's past mistakes, over and over again, which is why we must call for justice and a new way of life through the attributes of the heart, and without an attitude of being 'against'.

However, these simple guidelines for a new form of global activism should not be seen as vague or utopian thinking, but as a hard-headed strategy for how to fight and actually win: by engaging the hearts of millions of people in every country through peaceful mass demonstrations that are concerned with an immediate end to poverty-induced human suffering. Never before have we experienced such a profoundly moving and joyful spectacle on this planet in its fullest flourishing. Many activists now declare the possibility of creating a better world, but social transformation on the scale required can never be realised without engaging the attributes of the heart and mind in unison. Then human intelligence may begin to move in the right direction at long last—no longer towards profit, ideology or self-interest, but towards the common good of all with the primary consideration given to the least privileged among us.

***

What we need most today is not revolution but common sense, simplicity and wisdom to manifest in our everyday thinking and actions. Heralding *Article 25* is the direct way to bring these qualities into our protest activities, to the extent that it will lessen the tension between rich and poor and invite both to come around the table to talk, in both figurative and literal terms. Some people today are even calling for a 'spiritual revolution' which may appear to be along the correct line of thinking, but in reality it is vain and implausible to call for a sudden illumination of our collective consciousness when human relationships are based on want, confusion, ignorance, and identification with isms and ideologies.

What kind of spiritual revolution can we have in such a divided and materialistic society as ours, if not a 'commercialised spiritual revolution' as has already happened with the introduction of yoga teachings in the West? It is hopeless to try and bring about a spiritual revolution without first undergoing a psychological revolution across the whole of society, so that we may begin to know who we truly are through common association in popular demonstrations with the engagement of our hearts. Once every person on earth has what they need to live with self-respect, trust and freedom then perhaps we can ask for a planetary spiritual revolution, otherwise if we could personify that revolution it would say: 'I would love to come amongst you all, but I am incapable of doing so until you put your house in order first'.

There are many people who still strive for their own spiritual revolution within a world that is blighted by escalating inequalities, devastating wars and climate upheaval, in which circumstances our so-called enlightenment can only be attained as an individual who is perversely oblivious to the profounder spiritual crisis of our time. We may seek refuge in an ashram or monastery and meditate in isolation for many years, but what are we meditating for when the world is fast approaching an era of interminable social chaos and environmental catastrophe unless it dramatically changes direction? Besides, isn't feeding the hungry and serving our poorest brethren also a path to spiritual salvation? As long as the crime of hunger amidst plenty continues in the twentieth-first century there should be no talk whatsoever of a spiritual revolution, as far as the present writer is concerned, at least not before we have a planetary psychological revolution that leads us to herald *Article 25* with an attitude of 'what about the others?'

The fact of people demonstrating all over the world in this manner is itself a psychological revolution that will be realised through the joyful awareness that humanity is One, and the sound of those demonstrations will be magnetised in such a way that they will in fact constitute the very beginning of a spiritual revolution on this earth. A new uprising of constant worldwide demonstrations in the manner indicated above will give such dignity and strength to people that we will look at each other without barriers of language, race and class as if we were always brothers and sisters, and as if trust had always been there if only we had chosen to use it. Then we will know what it means to call ourselves an ambassador of humanity once *Article 25* begins to be implemented through new laws, policies, and global economic arrangements. At which time a strange phenomenon will take place in the minds of men and women with a previously unknown quality that stems from awareness of the other, a newfound respect and trust, and of course the energy that we call love.

What we have seen already in many protest encampments since 2011 is a small indication of this emergent consciousness, although those former events will pale into insignificance compared to our vision of many nations erupting with the same united demand. Have you observed how people behave when they interact as a group during the peaceful mass demonstrations of recent years, where there is a joy to be together and serve other people without thought of the 'me', even if it is just to share books in a makeshift library or distribute food for free? These activists typically share almost everything they have, and they experience a *joie de vivre* and a sense of solidarity that is inspiring, creative and healing in its expression. So the writer would like to ask the reader: should we regard this behaviour as merely 'hippy stuff', or does it signify the onset of a new age based on right human relations that perhaps you have already sensed yourself?

The events we have witnessed so far represent an unconscious appeal to bring a new way of life into being, and it is a sign of things to come on a hitherto unseen and planetary scale. Please imagine if you can the full release of this heart engaged phenomenon in every country of the world, as experienced and expressed by many millions of people for protracted months at a time. The sporadic waves of popular protest that have recently taken place are effectively saying 'we want a better world', but the instructions have now been given for how to inaugurate this better world that people everywhere are intuitively grasping for.

By heralding *Article 25*, we may also help create a universal awareness that sharing the world's resources is verily the solution to our civilisational crisis, for there is an interdependent relationship between these two conceptions that will be realised through continuous worldwide demonstrations with an engaged heart and massed goodwill. That relationship has always been simple but can only be described allegorically at the present time, since it is a long journey for man to realise who he is after countless lives until he begins to awaken from a deep slumber and perceive the simple truth of his divine potential. In the love of God or Life everything is simple, whereas only man makes everything complex through his ignorance, greed and attachment to isms.

Thus let us try to think symbolically of *Article 25* as the scout who goes off in search of a missing party, namely humanity, before guiding us back to his mothership which is the principle of sharing. It is in this sense that *Article 25* holds within itself the answer and the alternative, which will be revealed when humanity comes together and calls for it out loud in the midst of a universal psychological revolution. Then it will be as if a chemical reaction happens, like many test tubes uncorking and bubbling over all at once, until we experience the most unexpected revelation: that life is a precious gift and really worth living, for *humanity is One*. Then it won't be long before *Article 25* leads us home to the principle of sharing, and the reconstruction of our world can begin.

PART V

Education for a New Earth

If we declare and truly believe that another world is possible, then what are we going to do about our blindfolded politicians, our collective indifference and complacency, and all the isms that are preventing us from finding our way to truth and freedom? When are we going to look at each other without judgements, fear or condemnation, but with joy and goodwill? When are we going to experience a day that is different from every other day, if only for once in our short lives? Again the answer is a new kind of education based on Self-knowledge through love and wisdom, beginning with the revelation that humanity is One which is the liberating truth of life on earth, regardless of how long we have tried to deny it. Thus we may also correctly say that we don't need revolution today but right education, for there is no hope of implementing *Article 25* in perpetuity unless we learn to live more simply and equally within the means of one planet that everyone must share.

New educational methods are urgently necessary to sustain the laws that will guarantee the full realisation of *Article 25* around the world, because humanity is so conditioned by isms and centuries of wrong thinking about human nature that any such laws would otherwise not last for long. We generally have no idea what right education means in our dysfunctional societies, where a purported 'good education' is based on personality identification and the glamour of achieving a recognised measure of success. Consequently, our schools and universities have created many 'well educated' people in positions of power who are experts at wrecking the planet and other human beings. This is an undeniable fact that should be observed in relation to a society that is rapidly consuming the natural resource base that sustains life itself, while the extremes of poverty and wealth are growing to such an extent that they have within them the seeds of a third world war. Every prime minister, president or chief executive has had what may be described as a good education, and yet they all invariably perpetuate these disastrous trends.

When a privileged child goes to school they are in no sense educated in terms of right human relations, but are rather indoctrinated and conditioned by many centuries of erroneous understanding about the meaning and purpose of life, while being tragically contaminated in more recent times by the forces of commercialisation. A young child or teenager who engenders the highest aspirations about making the world a better place is destined to return at the end of their education with a mind that is not only conditioned but entirely contaminated by these forces, even if that young adult retains an undeterred ambition to 'give back to' society or pursue a public-spirited vocation.

We are all the children of an education that tells us how we should think, that indoctrinates us to achieve success, that cultures us to be ambitious and, as a consequence, divides us and ultimately produces destruction and abuse of the Self. Education as we know it today, even in many of the alternative and more spiritually-oriented schools or colleges, is increasingly like a factory that creates automatons who are programmed and mass-produced to become a successful 'somebody'. Hence we are all subject to an education that misleads us, that manipulates us and that fails to expand our conscious awareness about the true nature of our being, instilling us instead with an individualistic sense of ambition that leads to greed, selfishness, and eventually indifference to the suffering of others and the earth.

Humanity is eternal and indivisible in the one evolution and yet, as a result of our wrong identification with materiality, our wrong conditioning and our wrong educational methods, we have sunk to a point where many millions if not billions of people feel as if they are not part of their society, or that the world is somehow their enemy. In the same way as the activist often believes that the system is against them, the very poorest citizens often believe that they do not belong as a part of human civilisation. At the other extreme, for the person who attained a 'good education' and achieved a high social status through conforming to the selfish arts of commercialisation, they are conditioned to build a banner in their unconscious mind that reads: 'I am one of the few deserving individuals who made it'.

When we look holistically at the world situation from a spiritual understanding of the One Humanity, we may conclude that no person is properly educated in any school or university of whatever prestigious status. In a dysfunctional society that has chosen commercialisation as its nucleus, it is virtually impossible to educate a child in a spiritually wholesome and psychologically healthy way. What we are really producing is not a 'good education' through a cultured awareness of the inner Self, but rather an assembly line of 'good consumers'. We are not only bred to become consumers of endless commercialised products and services, but we are also cultivated to consume ourselves through the inadvertent abuse of our own lives. The person who doesn't think for themselves, who isn't equipped with Self-knowledge, who hasn't been taught to live and move in loving awareness, is the one who will consume the goods outwardly and consume themselves inwardly—which means we are better described not as a free and joyful human beings, but as 'self-commodities'. Instead of being creative with all the energy and beauty that we are endowed with in our environment, we prefer to remain asleep and complacent through our lack of inner awareness, and hence we 'consume' or dissipate our most precious human attributes and unknowingly suffer a slow spiritual starvation.

We are consuming ourselves in every conceivable way—politically, economically, socially, environmentally and emotionally—in everything from our innocent abuse of the natural world through mass patterns of unsustainable consumption, to the psychological self-destruction that follows from our greed, self-pity, depression, loneliness and addictive drug-taking. We are even 'self-consuming' through our indifference to all the suffering that is happening both within and without ourselves. That is why each day feels the same as every other day in its tiredness and turmoil, because we are all consuming our own humanity to some extent whether we are aware of it or not. And in the midst of all this social turmoil and self-inflicted violence, we still constantly search for our good health and an elusive happiness. Often, we search with such stubbornness that we are overwhelmed by sorrow and pain to the point that we believe it is necessary to sacrifice our own lives, which can be seen as a final sad attempt to annihilate the Self through the act of suicide.

In general, our political leaders have a confused and distorted view concerning the meaning of right human relationship, just like the rest of us who are self-induced to live in a world of beliefs, isms and ignorance. Surrounded by all the inequalities and misery of modern societies, to be the leader of a political party is actually a symbol of how humanity has divided itself due to the absence of an education that is based on Self-knowledge, one that can sustain loving awareness in the life of a child and lead to inner detachment and wisdom in young adulthood and beyond. Right education, in this sense, is antithetical to our present-day understanding of the term leadership, which has a debasing connotation of the higher and the lower, the one who leads and the many who must follow. For within that process of following, man has sunken into a prevalent state of complacency and indifference by denying his own spirituality, creativity and inborn intelligence. In any dysfunctional and morally degenerate society that idolises the selfish accumulation of material wealth and power, political leadership will only ever result in more confusion and social division, and can only ever lead to more repression, violence and widespread suffering.

What kind of democracy are we talking about while

clearly witnessing in our daily life how politics has become a vulgar game that denies the very idea and existence of the One Humanity, where every political candidate appears, as if from nowhere, in order to bestow their timeworn isms on our tired lives and our children? Following isms is itself an act of vulgarity, so who can blame the many people who don't want to engage with those politicians who are hungry for a powerful position, instead replying: 'Oh politics, I don't even want to hear that word!' The many other people who closely follow parties of the left or right also generally fail to think in terms of right human relationship and our innate spiritual unity, and are far more interested in seeing that their chosen party defeats all others in the latest political battle. They too are part of the vulgar game as much as the politicians, not least if they pledge their allegiance to an ism in the hope that a new leader will bring down their taxes or perhaps reduce their mortgage repayments, thereby reinforcing a complacent and insular way of life. Life and Self-knowledge have always been based on the growth of our awareness through human relationship, not on the confinement of our consciousness to those self-centred boxes that we call 'my life' or 'my rights'. Refusing to perceive this reality throughout our lives, we repeatedly deceive ourselves and others by believing that society can change for the better by replacing one political ism with another.

In these confused times, the fight for votes in a big election campaign creates even more stress and division within a nation, and on a psychological level the act of voting represents the increasing disunity and spiritual fragmentation of that society. This is not to dismiss the many historical struggles for universal suffrage and better democratic representation, but it is to look at these questions of democracy and leadership with a more holistic and spiritual faculty of perception. Who and what are we voting for when the economy is collapsing, when commercialisation is rampant in its abuse of man and nature, when the environment is deteriorating so quickly that it may eventually render the planet uninhabitable?

To merely vote for another ism of the left or right can only bring more pain and division from within this maelstrom, because it means we are still refusing to relinquish our complacency, expand our conscious awareness, and take responsibility for changing the world situation ourselves. We cannot blame the government for these issues if we voted for them in the first place, and then did nothing else. In this respect, the government doesn't only reflect what we have become, but also what we deserve. The government and the electorate are one and the same, including the apathetic or alienated non-voters who decline to be involved in the lavish and distracting palaver of electioneering. Yet for so long have we been stuck with an inadequate education and hence erroneous ideas of leadership that we seem to think this is the only way society can function. It appears that we cannot even imagine a different way of living based on right human relationship—without which, in reality, there can never be harmony or peace in world affairs.

As long as there are competitive and power-hungry leaders as we witness them today, there will always be conflict and social divisions. And as long as there are people who keep following these so-called leaders, there will always be the unconscious denial of our inborn spirituality, creativity and wisdom. But where there is love, where there is freedom, where there is respect and trust for the other without a mind conditioned by isms, then there is no authority or leadership; there is only guidance. True leadership guides, whereas leadership in its present form creates more and more followers, which is where the root of all our problems lies. Thus when everyone has Self-knowledge through right education—supposing that humanity can overcome a civilisational (or rather *spiritual*) crisis to reach this necessary stage for our continued evolution—then voting for a leader would almost be an impossibility, and there would be no further need for political parties. There would simply be a group of designated people who serve in government positions as representatives of the common good, selected not through votes but through public recognition of their wisdom and inclusive attitudes. And the first duty of any such representative would be to guarantee that all people have their basic material needs secured at all times, while also ensuring that everyone receives an education that equips them to grow in soul awareness and guide themselves within their own spiritual evolution through service to mankind.

The youth who come together in grassroots social movements are beginning to sense this new mode of being that will define the coming age. Already, they are naturally emerging without any clear leadership structure or centralised authority because they are learning for themselves how to think in terms of common sense through an engaged heart, and not on the basis of isms. Through their many experiments in popular empowerment and participatory democracy, they are rapidly discovering this revelatory truth: that we do not need leaders to govern society if everyone's consciousness is guided towards cooperating for the greatest good of the greatest number, thus equipping everyone to realise their own leadership potential in the pursuit of social justice and right human relations.

However, this new consciousness faces an enormous problem due to the nature of the system it challenges, one that is based on the old ways of self-interest, competition and partisan politics with the support of millions of followers in each country, including a privileged rich minority and powerful vested interests. How, then, can protesters achieve the backing of millions of people around the world, but without looking outwardly for leaders to direct their ideas and activities? The correct approach to initiating this mass civic engagement should warrant no further repetition: it requires us to activate our hearts and appeal to the wider public by heralding *Article 25* through non-stop peaceful demonstrations. We are sadly mistaken if we believe a better world will come about through the ballot box unless we also organise ourselves in huge coordinated protests, for there is no political leader in existence who is capable of doing the job for us even if they tried. And why should we vote for any politician who is not trying to educate the nation to think of those less fortunate than ourselves, both within our own country and abroad, especially if that means we are giving power to a political party to rule our lives?

These observations should not be read as an instruction to withdraw our support from mainstream democratic processes, but surely you too have asked yourself if voting in national elections is going to make a difference to the critical world situation. We could make a comparison between voting for a politician and recycling our household waste materials, for both activities are necessary and commendable but will have little impact in themselves on reversing calamitous global trends. Will recycling plastics be enough to mitigate the effects of global warming, and will your vote be enough to end hunger and impoverishment across the world? Obviously not, hence the only way to begin resolving these intractable problems is to go out on the streets and demonstrate continuously in massive gatherings, as proposed in the preceding chapter.

The real question we should ask ourselves is not why our governments are failing to save the world, but why are we failing to compel them to take appropriate action as our elected representatives? It may be true that no politician can overcome the control of an immoral and corrupt system by themselves, presuming that any world leader today is seriously inclined to promote the highest interests of humanity as a whole. But how many times have we demanded that the man or woman we vote for must prioritise an end to hunger and poverty as their foremost concern? From the perspective of *Article 25*, the only true presidents or prime ministers are those who are elected by the human heart and not the ballot box to serve the very poor, such as the committed workers in thousands of non-governmental organisations who do their best to provide healthcare, shelter, food and other necessities while our governments neglect to fulfil this vital role.

Furthermore, it is instructive to look at the meaning of democracy from the viewpoint of the person who lives on less than one dollar a day, and then to ask yourself what voting is going to achieve in your daily struggle to survive. Will you say 'My vote is my power and my right', or will you respond 'I don't care about democracy, I just want to eat!' As the citizen of a rich country, I may be so stuck in my self-interested concerns about lowering taxes, increasing my pension, controlling immigration and so on, that the only freedom I have is conferred to me by scheming politicians in business suits, which is the freedom to vote for any political ism I choose to—if that is what you mean by democracy and freedom. But as a desperately poor person in a remote village or shantytown, I am unlikely to be asked to vote at all unless I am bribed or coerced to by a duplicitous party candidate. If I live in India, for example, I am supposed to call my country the greatest democracy in the world, even though it also boasts the greatest number of undernourished people while spending over 40 billion dollars each year on armaments. Or perhaps I have never heard of the word democracy in my secluded and conflict-ridden community somewhere in Africa, where the only freedom conferred to me by wealthy politicians is the freedom to die in poverty without any government help.

So what kind of democracy are we talking about if we look at this question from a truly global and inclusive perspective, and with a spiritual understanding of the One Humanity? The capitalists are talking about democracy, the socialists are talking about democracy, even the fascists are talking about democracy today; but who is going to give the freedom to vote to the person who is dying of malnutrition—not a vote to elect another political party, but a vote to live? That is a vote that should have been given to that person by all of us, instead of focusing solely on our fight for justice and 'my rights' within our own country alone. The vote to live for the world's hungry will not be given by any politician, as we have hitherto established; it can only come from ordinary people in the streets through a concerted demand for implementing *Article 25*. And such a vote cannot be given through our apathy or indifference; it can only be granted through the engagement of our hearts, our compassion and our common sense. But isn't it true that we have failed to do that for many, many decades even though the horrific reality of life-threatening poverty has persisted throughout all these years? Then shame on us!

Let's observe very carefully the person who says 'it's the fault of my government for not taking action', instead of thinking that they should stand up and take action themselves. To again perceive this psychological tendency from the perspective of our spiritual unity and interconnectedness, the very act of blaming politicians when people are dying in poverty is to inwardly divide oneself from the rest of humankind, unless we also get involved to end this crime of needless impoverishment in a world of plentiful resources. Our collective complacency is even tacitly revealed in our use of language when we describe certain viruses as 'diseases of the poor', as if the poor are somehow different from us and responsible for creating these lethal maladies through their own imprudence. Are mass outbreaks of largely treatable diseases really the fault of the poor or the politicians, or are we all to blame through our complacent attitude to the preventable suffering of those people we do not know? Indeed if we had together demanded that *Article 25* were implemented as a law in every nation, then we could have long ago addressed the root causes of disease and health inequality in less developed countries. With adequate shelter, healthcare, sanitation and good nutrition for all of our poorest brothers and sisters, many fatal diseases may have been consigned to history instead of resurging in recent decades.

Such reflections may help to further suggest what we mean by thinking in terms of common sense, and what we mean by advocating for the principle of sharing to govern global economic affairs—which is not a simplistic idea, not a utopian proposition, but *where real life is*. The many aid organisations that try to assist the poor will always be overwhelmed in their task and eventually lose heart towards their work, until their efforts are boosted by sympathetic worldwide demonstrations that follow the common sense strategy of heralding *Article 25*. There are billions of people throughout the world who live in a state of continual struggle and privation, many of whom are ready to come out of their houses and protest for a very long period of time, if only they are invited to and given hope that their circumstances can change.

So let's get out on the streets and not question anymore what action we should take. And let's not vote for any politician unless ending hunger and poverty is at the top of their agenda, along with a pledge to cooperate with all other parties around the table for the good of the nation and all peoples everywhere. That is the common sense course of action for transforming the world, although how strange and sad it is that we have reached this stage when such an extreme measure is necessary to awaken sanity in political affairs. Just imagine that humanity is like a large dysfunctional family, and its many children are so mistreated and unloved that they are eventually forced to stand on the pavement and protest against their parents. What a sad and shocking indictment of that broken household, and what a sad way to look at what is happening on this planet from the most holistic and spiritual perspective.

Suppose we lived on a very peaceful and evolved planet where the scourge of hunger amidst plenty were unthinkable, what then would we make of the great divisions, recurrent conflicts and needless suffering that characterises life on earth? We wouldn't even need to land our spaceship on this beautiful and bounteous world, we would only need to look through giant binoculars to observe how its people are interacting with each other far below. If we saw just one violent protest on the streets it would mean 'don't visit!', for that would symbolise the division that exists between the governments and the people, as well as the spiritual imbalance that is prevalent across the planet as a whole. But if we saw millions upon millions of people gathered in peaceful demonstrations that express sharing, joy and goodwill, then it would mean 'keep watching!', for those united crowds would symbolise a planetary evolution that is coming of age, as revealed through a majority of the population that no longer wants to remain divided and is standing up for its poorest brethren. Thus it will only be a question of time before that planet completely reassesses the nature and purpose of its family relations, and finally implements the principle of sharing into its political affairs and global economic arrangements.

***

In summary, we may discern that there are two main solutions for resolving the world's converging crises: firstly, to share essential resources between nations through new forms of global exchange that are no longer motivated by profit, competition and self-interest. And secondly, to inaugurate a new education in the intervening years that can bring about the awareness that is needed to sustain this more cooperative, compassionate and simpler mode of living. In the twenty-first century, humanity already demonstrates an awareness of our interconnectedness and unity in so many ways, such as through the globalised trade in goods and services (however unbalanced and inequitable in its current form), or through worldwide communications and sport events that reveal our global integration and commonality of interests, and even through outpourings of grief and generosity following natural disasters with a great loss of life. A new education must build upon this nascent understanding of our planetary interdependency, to the point that every person in every nation realises the meaning and importance of sharing the world's resources with respect to achieving justice, peace and right human relations.

Children must be educated along these lines as part of their school curriculum to ensure they always think in terms of the One Humanity, meaning that they comprehend each nation's unique contribution to the whole and each individual's inherent equality and creative potential. There is also a type of education based on love and wisdom that can help a young person to realise 'who am I in this world', just as schooling is necessary to comprehend the social and natural sciences, the humanities, the arts and so forth. By this means it is possible to train a child to keep the mind calm and the heart always awake in human relationship through Self-awareness, although it is not the present writer's place to give precise details as to what specific form such an education should take. Suffice it to say that no religious beliefs, political ideologies or 'isms' of any type should be imposed on a child's mind in their formative stages of learning and development. Furthermore, a special or complementary syllabus should be introduced within every school that teaches a young person how to think of others without self-centredness, and how to serve the common good in a world where the primacy of profit-making and individualistic competition is consigned to the past.

How fast or slowly this new education is introduced crucially depends on the concurrent economic and political reforms that must take place on a worldwide basis, for which reason school lessons should initially include basic teachings on how the principles of sharing and cooperation are the foundation of a sustainable global economic system. All children should be guided to understand the subjective interrelationship of human beings with each other and the natural environment, and the consequent importance of sharing the world's accumulated wealth, resources, technology and knowledge more equally and freely among nations. Like a family naturally shares what it has among its members, so must the family of nations arrange its affairs in such a way that surplus resources are given over in trust to some form of global pool, and redistributed according to need on the basis of sharing rather than profit or greed. Such a straightforward concept could not be simpler, and it may one day represent the most elementary introduction to the meaning of right relationship between the world's peoples and countries. If we can believe that the principle of sharing in its truest expression will underlie an international economic system of the near future, perhaps none of our youngest generation—no longer conditioned by outmoded ideologies and isms—will engender any ambition to be a leading politician when they eventually graduate. Although if a child does grow up to be a president or prime minister, they would know exactly how to ensure their nation lives in peace with all other nations.

By reflecting upon the preceding observations in their entirety, again we may deduce that the world's problems are so complex and yet so simple to resolve. Through systematically implementing the principle of sharing into our societies and international affairs, in turn that will necessitate the reconstruction and simplification of our global economic framework. In turn, it will also necessitate the inauguration of a new education based on right human relations in order to sustain this simpler and more enlightened social order. All this begins with heralding *Article 25 en masse* which is the necessary foundation for the political and economic transformations that must urgently follow, from which understanding *Article 25* is not calling for 'human rights' to be realised but truly the commencement of right human relations on this earth. When these essential conditions are firmly established for all people over many successive generations, *Article 25* may not even be mentioned anymore but only remembered by historians as 'the Article of common sense'.

In symbolic terms, humanity is suffering from a potentially fatal sickness called separation and the sole remedy is the ageless principle of sharing, which is for one reason beyond all others. For once this world shares its resources and every person has their basic needs permanently secured, our present modes of education will inevitably, and perhaps dramatically, begin to change their form and overall direction. Amidst all the social, psychological and political chaos of these days, the principle of sharing can bring about an ineffable wave of change if only by awakening a silent educator that exists within all of us—that is, the loving inner guidance that can lead an individual to respect themselves and no longer consume their own humanity through self-destructive patterns and behaviours, in accordance with the inner and outer meanings of consumption that we earlier discussed. In the same way that quarrelling neighbours can find peace and change inwardly by sharing among themselves, the process of sharing resources on a global scale has the potential to change the collective consciousness of humanity in a way that is presently unimaginable. From the micro level to the macro, sharing has the ability to reverse the coin by turning selfish competition into selfless cooperation, social division into common union, disorder into balance and equilibrium, and hatred into love.

Humanity will be freely inspired to begin a new era of education based on right human relations when such changes are sweeping the world, both inwardly and psychologically as well as outwardly across society. Hence there are two forms of right relationship that we should consider with respect to both the individual and their social environment, for when there is right relationship within oneself then a person is naturally guided towards right relationship with others. By verifying this factual reality through inner contemplation and outer observation we may further reaffirm the immense importance of implementing *Article 25*, as this is the shadow of the principle of sharing that will ultimately bring balance into the mayhem of destructive self-consumption as previously defined, thereby opening the doors to living more simply, sustainably and peacefully in relation to each other and the natural world.

When pondering the meaning of right human relations it is also helpful to conceive of the principle of sharing as a great social physician or planetary psychotherapist, one that has the power to heal in almost every possible way—by feeding the hungry and curing the diseased, mending broken families and restoring mental health, rebuilding communities and nurturing individuals to regain their confidence and creativity, and so on without end. So if you want to heal yourself as an individual or as a group, advocate for the principle of sharing to be implemented into world affairs and serve humanity by heralding *Article 25* with every ounce of energy you have, thus decentralising yourself from the disease called separation and playing your part in establishing a new earth based on right human relations.

***

The reader may still question how millions of people can be persuaded to gather on the streets in the manner suggested, to which the writer can only reply that the responsibility for answering this question lies with the readers themselves. No further instructions can be given as to 'how' to bring about these peaceful mass protests, other than to recommend that we personally examine from all sides the meaning and potential of heralding *Article 25* as a viable strategy for world transformation. One spark is all that may be needed when the time has come, just like the idea of proclaiming the power of 'the 99%' was sparked by one individual at an opportune moment. And the time is soon coming—nay, is already here—to revive *Article 25* within the United Nations by demonstrating around the world on this precise basis.

However, a response to this question of 'how?' can also be answered very simply; we just need to awaken the hearts of ordinary people and that is all, for within each and every human heart is embedded the love and wisdom of all humanity. If a rich person looks anew at the world and inwardly observes: 'My God, there is so much money and wealth everywhere, and yet there are so many people who are dying in poverty!', then that banal observation itself represents the beginning of wisdom as realised through the engagement of the heart. And if that person commits to sharing their wealth for the purpose of relieving human suffering, then that act itself represents a small manifestation of love and wisdom in this world. The heart with its attributes is always simple and yet very, very wise for it is capable of leading us to recognise who we truly are as human beings despite all of our complacency, indifference and mind conditioning.

What is needed to awaken the hearts of millions of people towards the needs of others is trust, inspiration and joy, which are all qualities that will be brought about when enough nations come together with the same selfless concern to end hunger and life-threatening poverty. Then we will know that many of the activists who are fighting for justice today—such as those who work within the various networks of aid agencies, civil society organisations and progressive political groups—are unconsciously calling for sharing through the implementation of *Article 25*. So if it is a spark that is needed to awaken the attributes of the human heart (namely love and wisdom as expressed through compassion, empathy, generosity, sharing and so on), then it is the spark of intelligence freed from conditioning that says: 'Let's end hunger and poverty once and for all because now the time has finally come, and we can really do it if enough people get involved!'

The fact is that most ordinary citizens are heavily conditioned and unaware of the critical world situation, although even to know the overwhelming extent of human deprivation and then do nothing about it is unfortunately part of our conditioning. Thus what else can be said in response to the question 'how will this begin?', except to say 'by using your intuition and common sense, and then more common sense!' A large portion of humanity is now ready to hear the call, so let's recognise that we are all fighting for the same cause and unite via the engagement of our hearts, and let *Article 25* bring us again the joy of living, the joy of being creative, the joy of realising at last that humanity is One.

We appear to have reached a stage where we are so confused that this question of 'how' is lost in the myriad conflicting answers from political factions and countless speculative theories. Any activist who declares 'another world is possible' is incapable of navigating all this divisive thinking to produce a comprehensive and workable strategy for planetary transformation. Hence it may be true that another world is possible, but not without common sense (freed of isms and ideologies) and the engagement of our hearts among enormous numbers of other people. Yet we have refused to listen to our hearts for so long that the world situation is fast approaching a catastrophic climax from which it seems as if only divine intervention may indeed save us, considering how man has led himself into a cul-de-sac through his own arrogance and recklessness until even the weather is almost beyond repair.

Somewhat incongruously, the religious elders in the numberless churches, synagogues, mosques and temples of the world could have always promulgated this urgent message to engage our hearts and save the dying poor, instead of spending all their time in gathering a flock or seeking refuge in a sacred ism. We might ask why it's so difficult for the Church to talk unremittingly about the injustice of hunger in a world of plenty, for example, thus educating their congregation to heal the world instead of exclusively worshipping Mary and Jesus, and thereby heeding the contemporary relevance of the Christ's simple teaching.[14] One could argue that the Church should all along have educated humanity in how to engage the heart and serve others, a role that it has largely renounced amidst all the dogma, schisms and hypocritical scandals of its ignominious history. Now as always, there is no psychological difference between the politician and the priest when both are motivated by thought of power or personal privilege, to the extent that one yearns to make their name in history while the other yearns to become a 'chosen one' in the eyes of God. With all our knowledge of the alarming scale of human deprivation that needlessly exists today, it is fair to say that no politician or priest has any idea of true public service or compassion in the name of Jesus unless every second of their day is occupied in trying to implement the principle of sharing in their communities, countries and most importantly among all nations.

If we can imagine that the Christ returns to the modern

world as foretold and dramatically declares Himself on our television screens, it is interesting to contemplate what His divine advice might be to governments and humanity at large. Would He talk in complex academic terms about destroying capitalism and creating a socialist alternative, or would He call upon our hearts to think about others and immediately save the starving millions? Would He advise us to share with our neighbours and within our own communities alone, or would He counsel us to share the resources of the world on the basis of justice, compassion and right human relations? Perhaps His advice would be very plain and simple despite His consummate knowledge of humanity's problems, wisely understanding as He would that implementing *Article 25* is the antidote for a divided world that is held in thrall to the battle of isms and commercialisation.

But how many people do we think would follow His advice? How many would be outraged by His humble instruction to share and save our world? And how many would remain indifferent to His heartrending words, even if they were embraced by the Christ's love in a universal experience of the Pentecost? Of all these three reactions it is the last one that should concern us the most, because at least the person who disagrees is thinking for themselves and may be open to changing their mind. A complacent response is far more disturbing, however, because it represents the ingrained indifference that has permeated society and held back human evolution for thousands of years. We may speculate that the Gods have gotten used by now to man's inhumanity to man, but They have never gotten used to our collective complacency and indifference that enables history to repeat itself again and again. From Their divine perspective, perhaps this is the real reason why the bloody conflicts and gross injustices are passed down from each generation and perpetually continue.

Unfortunately, these imaginings lead us to an ominous conclusion when the few major precedents we have for whole societies uniting on behalf of the greater good is through a great war or total economic breakdown. If it is true that in order to transform the world we must first engage the hearts of innumerable people with the same united cause, then history suggests there are actually two World Saviours that may be capable of initiating this colossal task. While many spiritually-inclined people may place their hope in a return of the Christ, the fifth Buddha, the Imam Mahdi or Krishna, others may logically conclude that a final downfall of the global economy is necessary, to such an extent that it is no longer possible to continue in our old selfish and competitive ways of the past. Indeed when people are forced to survive by helping one another and sharing what they have, it is easy to realise that a different way of living is possible without remaining psychologically separated and divided in our social relationships. Even if we share just a single tin of sardines with someone else in need, there is still a movement of joy to be felt in that simple act of giving and receiving. And as a bonus, those people who share among themselves out of necessity and lack of choice may unexpectedly sense the perfume of peace within their community, however short-lived or small-scale is this inevitable result. For the principle of sharing is always associated with joy and peace, in whatever context it is applied—from the community level upwards to the international.

Thus perhaps we need an extended economic collapse

of global proportions to shake us out of our conditioning, to overcome our indifference to the suffering of those less fortunate than ourselves, and to awaken our hearts to the anguish of millions of people who are constantly deprived of access to essential resources. Perhaps we must collectively take a fall before we can stand up together and begin to traverse the right path, because we are always spurred to action through drama and catastrophe if not in response to common sense appeals to our reason and compassion. In other words, perhaps it isn't just love that humanity needs but a formidable crisis due to the combined apathy and unconcern that we have demonstrated throughout all these years, wherein we have been conditioned to seek our personal happiness and security at all costs even when the world is slowly falling apart around us.

Yet we are still so conditioned by the old ways of thinking that we may again revert to pursuing our materialistic and insular way of life, presuming the economy can return to its former state of growth and apparent stability. Even today, many protest marches and social movements are not concerned about transforming the world for the benefit of all, but are rather fighting for their national government to take them back to how they used to live before—caring nothing for the systemic injustices that maintain the stark inequalities among rich and poor. These complacent responses once more reveal how the ordinary citizen is as much to blame for society's problems as the politician, since the government at least someway reflects the same mentality that pervades a broad section of the overall public consciousness. Let's not forget that politicians are merely human beings who generally remain sincere in their intentions whatever ideology they promote, and it is the populace that sustains their polarised thinking through a tribe-like adherence to political isms of opposing sorts.

In this fact alone lies the greatest danger of our times, for a significant crash of the global economy could eventually lead to violence and revolution if different factions within some societies seek to depose those who remain in power. Let's also not forget that a riotous uprising of the public is extremely dangerous due to the vast state machinery that is prepared for this anticipated occurrence in countries of both the Global North and South, with the wholesale support of leading politicians and controlling financial interests. Hence if enough people violently protest against their government following another breakdown of the international economic system, then we can expect social unrest or even more outbreaks of civil war as we have painfully observed within the Middle East since 2011, where various factions or 'isms' that opposed an authoritarian leadership eventually started fighting against each other.

The only peaceful way to reorient the volatile world situation is so simple that it must be repeated once again: by engaging the attributes of the heart in massive worldwide protests without thought of ideology or self-interest, because the human heart when activated is infinitely wise and incapable of being 'against'. The pioneering youth are already attuning to this new energy that is flooding the world, and they know the time has come to move away from the old consciousness that says 'this is mine and not yours', 'you are black and I am white', 'it's not in the interests of our country', or 'you must live each day like every other day'. This fast emerging and unifying consciousness gives us much reason to hope for the future, although the fiercely progressive views of many youthful activists pose a further danger to society if they are not recognised and listened to very carefully by those who represent our long inglorious past.

The day of reckoning is near, so how shall we decide to usher in this new and better world? Are we going to use socialism? Are we going to use anarchy? Are we going to use religion? Or are we going to peacefully unite in uncountable numbers until our governments commit to sharing the resources of the world? A single demonstration will never work. A hundred marches on separate days will probably achieve relatively little. But millions upon millions of protests happening simultaneously around the world on the consistent basis of implementing *Article 25*, and continuing daily without cessation? That might just be enough.

Endnotes

1   For more information about Share The World's Resources, please visit: <www.sharing.org/about-us>

2   For a full list of publications in this ongoing series, please visit: <www.sharing.org/information-centre/articles/studies-principle-sharing>

3   For more on this subject, see: Mohammed Mesbahi, '*A discourse on isms and the principle of sharing*', Share The World's Resources, July 2014. <www.sharing.org/information-centre/articles/discourse-isms-and-principle-sharing>

4   See note 2.

5   cf. Mohammed Mesbahi, '*A discourse on isms*', op cit.

6   cf. Mohammed Mesbahi, '*Commercialisation: the antithesis of sharing*', Share The World's Resources, April 2014. <www.sharing.org/information-centre/articles/commercialisation-antithesis-sharing>

7   Mohammed Mesbahi, '*Rise up America, rise up!*', Share The World's Resources, October 2014. <www.sharing.org/information-centre/articles/rise-america-rise>

8   For example, see: Mohammed Mesbahi, '*Uniting the people of the world*', Share The World's Resources, May 2014. <www.sharing.org/information-centre/articles/uniting-people-world>

9   Willy Brandt, *North-South: A Program for Survival* (The Brandt Report), MIT Press, 1980; Willy Brandt, *Common Crisis, North – South: Co-Operation for World Recovery*, The Brandt Commission 1983. London: Pan 1983.

10 Share The World's Resources, *Financing the global sharing economy*, October 2012. <www.sharing.org/information-centre/reports/financing-global-sharing-economy>

11 Willy Brandt, op cit.

12 Editor's note: Following The Brandt Commission's proposals, leaders of eight industrialised and 14 developing nations gathered in Cancun, Mexico, in October 1981 for a summit aimed at breaking the deadlock in years of protracted negotiations on problems of world poverty. The hope was that representative heads of state would meet in an informal setting for two days, thereby creating the momentum and goodwill that would permit global negotiations to advance. In the end, however, no firm proposals materialised and the demands of Southern countries for a global reallocation of resources remained unmet. US President Ronald Reagan notably rejected the summit's aims to bridge the wealth gap between the few industrialised nations and the majority of poorer countries. While not all of the Brandt Commission's recommendations remain appropriate today (particularly its emphasis on increased trade liberalisation and global Keynsian policies in an era when we are fast approaching environmental limits), there is still much that policymakers and civil society campaigners can draw from its "program of priorities" and its vision for a more equitable world. Above all, this includes the proposed five-year Emergency Programme that would necessitate massive resource transfers to less developed countries and far-reaching agrarian reforms. The Commission also called for a new global monetary system, a new approach to development finance, a coordinated process of disarmament, and a global transition away from dependence on non-renewable energy sources. To date, governments have yet to realise Brandt's vision of a multilateral process for "discussing the entire range of North-South issues among all

the nations, with the support and collaboration of the relevant international agencies" (Common Crisis, 1983).

13 Mohammed Mesbahi, '*Rise up America, rise up!*', op cit.

14 cf. Mohammed Mesbahi, '*Christmas, the system and I*', Share The World's Resources, December 2013. <www.sharing.org/information-centre/articles/christmas-system-and-i>

The Author

Mohammed Mesbahi is a writer, political activist and founder of Share The World's Resources (STWR), a civil society organisation based in London, UK, with consultative status at the Economic and Social Council of the United Nations. For more information about STWR visit www.sharing.org.